ACCOUNTING FOR RESEARCH AND DEVELOPMENT EXPENDITURES

ACCOUNTING
RESEARCH
STUDY NO. 14

ACCOUNTING FOR RESEARCH AND DEVELOPMENT EXPENDITURES

By Oscar S. Gellein, M.S., CPA
and
Maurice S. Newman, Ph.D., CPA

Partners

Haskins & Sells

Published by the
American Institute of Certified Public Accountants, Inc.
666 Fifth Avenue   New York, New York   10019

*Copyright 1973 by the
American Institute of Certified Public Accountants, Inc.
666 Fifth Avenue, New York, N. Y. 10019*

Notice to Readers

The activities of the Accounting Principles Board and its research arm, the Accounting Research Division, which was created in 1959, will terminate June 1973. The series of accounting research studies, the first of which was published in 1961, will terminate in 1973 with the publication of the fifteenth study. Research studies authorized and assigned to authors prior to 1973 and not published in the accounting research series have been transferred to the AICPA's newly created Technical Research Division. This division was created by the AICPA to continue research on financial and reporting matters to support its positions before the new Financial Accounting Standards Board. All technical research activities of the Institute are consolidated in the new division.

D. R. Carmichael, Director
Technical Research

Publication of this study by the American Institute of Certified Public Accountants does not in any way constitute official endorsement or approval of the conclusions reached or the opinions expressed.

Contents

                                      Page

DIRECTOR'S STATEMENT ix

AUTHORS' PREFACE xi

Chapter

1. INTRODUCTION AND SUMMARY 1

    Accounting Problems, 1
        Definition of Research and Development, 2
        Deferral or Immediate Recognition, 2
        Amortization, 2
        Disclosure, 3
    Scope of Study, 3
    Research Methodology, 4
        Questionnaire, 4
        Interviews, 5
    Summary of Conclusions, 5
        Definition and Classification, 6
        Deferral or Immediate Recognition, 6
        Amortization, 8
        Disclosure, 8

2. HISTORICAL PERSPECTIVE 9

    Early Years, 9
        Lone Inventor, 9
        National Research Laboratories, 10
        Company Laboratories, 10
        Early Accounting, 10
    Middle Years, 11
        Growth in Research, 12
        Accounting Developments, 13
    Recent Years, 16
        Increasing Expenditures by Industry, 16

Chapter

    Increasing Personnel, 17
    Effect on the National Economy, 17
    Postwar Accounting Trend, 17
  Court Decisions in Tax Cases, 19
  Survey of Current Practice, 20
    *Distinguishing Research and Development
      from Production and Selling, 21*
    Distinguishing Research from Development, 21
    Immediate Recognition vs. Deferral, 21
    Disclosure, 22
    Classification in the Income Statement, 22
  Summary, 23

3. DEFINING RESEARCH AND DEVELOPMENT 24

  Composition of Research and Development Costs, 24
  Need for an Accounting Definition, 25
    Conflicts in Definitions, 26
    *Distinguishing Development Costs from
      Production Costs, 26*
    Excluding Technical Support, 26
    Disclosure in Financial Statements, 27
  Existing Definitions, 27
    NSF Definitions, 27
      Basic research, 29
      Applied research, 29
      Development, 29
    Other Definitions, 29
      Concept of a spectrum, 29
      Alternative bases of defining types, 30
      People, 31
      Place, 32
      Purpose, 33
      Process, 33
      Proceeds, 34
  Problems in Distinguishing Types, 35
    Conflicts in Concepts, 35
      Development of Pyroceram, 36
      Discovery of Vitamin B_{12}, 36
  Business and Accounting Definitions, 37
    Business Definition, 37

Chapter	Page

Accounting Definition, 38
  Costs included, 38
  Costs excluded, 39
  Distinguishing from production, 39
Subclassifications, 41

4. RESEARCH AND DEVELOPMENT PROGRAMS 43

Kinds of Programs, 43
  Continuing Research, 43
  Substantial Development Projects, 44
  New-Product Development Divisions, 44
  Development Stage Companies, 45
Refinement for Accounting Analysis, 45
Features of Continuing Research Programs, 46
  Composition, 46
  Concentration, 47
  Personnel Costs, 47
  Uncertain Prospects and Delays, 48
  Stable Percentage of Successful Projects, 48
  Possible Correlation Between Expenditures
     and Sales, 49
Features of Substantial Development Projects, 49
  Principal Differences, 50
  Prospects of Recovering Costs, 51
  Case Study—Development of Jet Aircraft, 52

5. THEORETICAL CONSIDERATIONS 55

Present Generally Accepted Accounting Principles, 55
  Concepts and Principles, 56
  Initial Recording, 56
  Realization Principle and Cost Allocation, 56
  Expense Recognition, 57
  Product Costs and Period Costs, 57
    Product costs, 58
    Period costs, 58
  Conservatism, 59
  Summary of General Theory, 60
Practical Problems, 60
  Associating Costs with Revenue, 60
  Classifying as Product or Period Costs, 61

Chapter *Page*

    Business-Preserving Costs, 61
       Necessary Costs, 62
       Optional Timing of Costs, 62
    Associating Business-Preserving Costs with Revenue, 63
       Objection to Present Practice, 63
       Deferring Business-Preserving Costs, 63
         Arguments for deferral, 63
         Arguments against deferral, 64
         Arbitrary deferral, 64
       Implications of Concept, 64

6. RECOMMENDED ACCOUNTING 66

    Continuing Research, 66
       Deferral or Immediate Recognition, 67
       Conclusion for Continuing Research, 68
    Substantial Development Projects, 69
       Uncertainty, 69
       Inability to Determine Recoverability of Costs, 69
       Need to Defer, 70
       Criteria for Deferral, 70
         Identifying a substantial development project, 71
         Formal approval, 71
         Technical feasibility, 71
         Timing, 72
         Reasonable probability of revenue, 72
         Applicable costs, 73
         Specific deferral, 73
         Excess costs, 73
       Amortization of Deferred Costs, 73
       Conclusions for Substantial Development Projects, 74
    Disclosure in Financial Statements, 74
       Continuing Research, 74
       Substantial Development Projects, 75

Appendix

    RESULTS OF A SURVEY OF ACCOUNTING PRACTICES 77

SELECTED BIBLIOGRAPHY 115

Director's Statement

Statistics cited in this study document the significance of industrial research and development in U.S. industry and the growth in expenditures for that purpose by U.S. companies over the past quarter century. Accounting for and disclosing the effects of research and development activities often affect substantially the financial position and results of operations of companies.

Financial reporting of research and development costs has been criticized because of accepted alternative accounting procedures and because of variations among companies in the extent and manner of disclosure of the effects of research and development costs. Disparate definitions of research and development activities have caused problems in both accounting and disclosure. For example, two companies that appear to disclose comparable costs might in fact not be comparable because one defines research and development much more broadly than the other.

Messrs. Gellein and Newman began the study at the invitation of Paul Grady, my predecessor, but it has been my pleasure to work with them through most of the study. They have been most cooperative and persevering. I express my appreciation to them and to their firm, Haskins & Sells, for this contribution to the accounting research program of the American Institute of Certified Public Accountants. I also wish to recognize the contribution to the study of Thomas W. McRae, my colleague on the staff of the accounting research division.

I am also grateful to members of the project advisory committee, who attended more meetings and reviewed more drafts than most committees. They gave valuable counsel and helpful suggestions throughout the study. All members of the committee favor publication of the study. No member contributed comments to be published in it. Approval of publication or absence of published comments by a committee member should not be interpreted as concurrence with the contents, conclusions, or recommendations of the study.

Due to changes in Institute organization, described in Notice to Readers, this study will be one of the last accounting research studies. However, I invite interested individuals and groups to read the study carefully and submit comments on it to

>D. R. Carmichael, Director
>Technical Research
>American Institute of CPAs
>666 Fifth Avenue
>New York, New York 10019

Comments submitted will be most useful if they cover not only the conclusions but also the analyses, premises, and arguments and if they include supporting reasons. The study and all comments received will be sent to the Financial Accounting Standards Board.

New York, N. Y.　　　　　　　　Reed K. Storey
February 1973　　　　　　　　　*Director of Accounting Research*

Authors' Preface

Having the privilege to probe an important area of accounting knowledge, such as the accounting treatment of research and development, requires a special combination of opportunity, time, and resources. We are grateful to Paul Grady, then Director of Accounting Research of the American Institute of Certified Public Accountants, for asking us to undertake the project and to Reed K. Storey, his successor, for his continued advice and counsel. We also appreciate the understanding support of our partners in Haskins & Sells, without which this study would not have been completed.

We wish to acknowledge the particular contribution of the members of the project advisory committee who were unstinting of their time in making useful suggestions about the organization and scope of the study and in offering constructive criticism at various draft stages. The members of the project advisory committee are: John W. Queenan, Chairman, Mortimer J. Fox, Jr., Howard L. Letts, John W. Nicholson, R. Russel Pippin, Walter R. Staub, and John Arch White.

We received substantial help from many sources such as members of the Industrial Research Institute, the American Accounting Association, the National Association of Accountants, the Department of Defense, the Securities and Exchange Commission, and the Bureau of the Budget. Many corporate executives in both the research and financial areas and many public accountants also gave freely of their time to discuss the nature of research and development. To these many unnamed people we express our thanks.

We received considerable help from Thomas W. McRae in editing and rewriting the final draft. We also acknowledge the invaluable assistance of Martin Mellman of the Bernard M. Baruch College of the City University of New York, and Eleanor Foley of the AICPA in reviewing the draft and checking references, and of our secretaries, Kitty Hamilton and Genevieve Rodd, for countless retypings of the manuscript.

We chose to build our analysis within the existing framework of accounting concepts and conventions. We did so in recognition of the importance of consistency of practice within a framework at any given time. We also recognize, however, the need for continuing attention to the framework itself as circumstances and needs for financial information change. As the objectives of financial statements are modified and the accounting framework accordingly is changed, we would see a need for reexamining the accounting for research and development expenditures.

We are also impressed with the obvious effect of research and development expenditures on economic growth. The potential contribution of scientists, engineers, and others concerned with industrial and related research goes beyond the descriptive possibilities of accounting.

New York, N.Y., February 1973   OSCAR S. GELLEIN
and
MAURICE S. NEWMAN

1
Introduction and Summary

During the past twenty years, business managers throughout the world have become increasingly aware of the contributions of research and development to an industrial economy. The officers and directors of most large companies in the United States and of many smaller ones now appreciate the part that technological innovation plays in their companies. Moreover, businessmen, legislators, accountants, and economists realize that expenditures for research and development are vital to industrial activity, to national defense, to corporate profits, and to the full employment of our national resources. Accounting for research and development costs, which was a matter of concern to only a few accountants two decades ago, is now the concern of most accountants, businessmen, and users of financial statements and a topic of sufficient complexity and urgency to warrant an accounting research study.

Accounting Problems

Certain decisions are as essential in determining accounting principles for research and development as in determining accounting principles for inventories or other items. The basic questions to be answered within the financial accounting system now followed in the United States are (1) what activities should be described as research and development in financial statements? (2) should a portion of research and development costs be deferred? (3) how should deferred costs be amortized? and (4) what information pertaining to research and development should be disclosed in financial statements? While those questions often seem exceedingly difficult, they must nevertheless be answered if accounting for research and development costs is to be improved. The ramifications of those questions are summarized in this section.

Definition of Research and Development. Some of the problems in accounting for research and development costs can be attributed to the absence of a satisfactory definition of research and development for accounting purposes. The extent to which expenditures are classified as research and development may affect the measurement of periodic net income under present accounting conventions. The available evidence indicates that expenditures that some companies classify as research and development are classified by other companies as either production or selling costs. Frequently, the costs of technical support—work performed by research scientists or engineers in support of production or sales—are classified as research and development costs. The extent to which costs of technical support are classified as research and development costs is difficult to determine, but comparative analysis of financial statements both between companies or over periods may lose much of its meaning if classification of expenditures by function varies.

Deferral or Immediate Recognition. The most important financial accounting problem for this study is to determine the portion, if any, of expenditures for research and development that should be deferred and associated with the future revenue expected to result from the expenditure and the portion that should be recognized as expenses when incurred. Generally accepted accounting principles require revenue to be recognized when realized and costs to be associated with related revenue. Thus, costs incurred in one period to produce an expected benefit in a future period are expenses of the future period and should therefore be deferred. In theory, costs deferred to future periods need not necessarily be assigned to specific products as costs of inventory but may be merely assigned to the related future period. In other words, the deferral of costs to a future period is intended to permit association of the total costs of the period with the total revenue of the period, although the costs may or may not be attributed to specific products.

Amortization. If costs of research and development are deferred, a corollary problem is to determine the method of amortization and the period of amortization. The difficulties of the problem are accentuated because deferred research and development costs are intangible assets that do not always have a clearly determinable life. A similar problem arises in accounting for the cost of a patent except that a patent has a life limited by law. The problem, however, may be more or less the same for deferred research and development costs as it is for a patent because the useful life of a patent may be shorter than its legal life.

Disclosure. Another financial reporting problem important to both preparers and users of financial statements is that of determining the type and amount of information pertaining to research and development that should be disclosed in financial statements. Present disclosure practice is mixed. Some companies disclose information pertaining to research and development, but both the type of information and the method of disclosing it may vary. Many companies do not disclose information on their research and development activities in their financial statements.

The problem for this study is not only to determine the desirability of disclosure but also the methods of disclosure. If disclosure is desirable, then questions arise as to whether companies should classify research and development expenses separately in the income statement and whether the amount should be included in the cost of sales or shown separately as an expense deducted from gross profit.

Scope of Study

The study is limited to the problems of accounting for research and development costs financed by industrial companies. It therefore covers company-financed research performed by commercial laboratories or colleges and universities but does not cover company-conducted research financed by federal or state agencies. Although expenditures for the exploration of minerals, petroleum, and other natural resources—ordinarily described in the industries involved as development costs—share many of the characteristics of expenditures for research and development, and similar accounting principles may apply, accounting for development costs in the extractive industries is covered in a separate accounting research study[1] and is therefore excluded from this study.

Since the study is confined to accounting problems of going concerns, it contains no formal conclusions on accounting for research and development expenditures of a development stage company. The

---

[1] Robert E. Field, *Accounting Research Study No. 11*, "Financial Reporting in the Extractive Industries" (New York: American Institute of Certified Public Accountants, Inc., 1969).

going concern assumption does not apply to a development stage company because it is usually speculative or promotional and has not realized a significant amount of revenue from the sale of products or services. The SEC prescribes specific conditions that a company must meet to file a registration statement as a development stage company and requires the company to file special purpose financial statements because general purpose statements are usually not suitable to describe its financial position. The practical problems of accounting for all expenditures of development stage companies are complex and involve considerations sufficiently unique to justify separate examination.

Research Methodology

The initial step in the research was to examine the pertinent literature to determine applicable theory and to obtain background information on the increasing significance of research and development in industry and the historical development of accounting concepts and principles related to research and development costs. The next step was to discuss current principles and practices with financial analysts, bankers, members of industry associations, accounting educators, and others. Finally, accounting practices were surveyed to ascertain, insofar as possible, the factors that led companies to account for research and development costs as they do. The survey was based on (a) a review of stockholders' reports and prospectuses of a large number of companies, (b) an extensive analysis of questionnaires completed by companies that spend relatively large amounts for research and development, and (c) interviews with representatives of companies that have a long history of conducting research and development programs.

Questionnaire. The Accounting Research Division (ARD) of the American Institute of Certified Public Accountants (AICPA) engaged Elmo Roper and Associates to assist in the preparation and tabulation of a questionnaire that was designed to elicit information necessary for the study but not available elsewhere. The ARD distributed the questionnaires to two groups of companies. The first group consisted of 300 major companies reported to be those with the largest amounts of company-financed expenditures for research and development.[2] The

---

[2] National Science Foundation, *Basic Research, Applied Research, and Development in Industry, 1964* (Washington, D.C.: U.S. Government Printing Office, 1966), p. 32.

second group consisted of 100 research-oriented companies considered to have passed through the development stage some time during the past 25 years. The second group was selected to determine whether significant differences existed between the practices of those companies and the practices of the 300 major companies included in the first group.

The ARD received responses to the questionnaire as follows:

	Size of Sample	Number Responding	Percent of Total
First group	300	209	70%
Second group	100	36	36
Total	400	245	61%

The rate of response for the first group and the total sample exceeded normal expectations for a questionnaire survey, particularly since the questionnaire was complex and time-consuming to answer. The Appendix contains the text of the questionnaire and a statistical analysis of the responses.

Interviews. Many company officials responsible for finance and accounting and some responsible for research were interviewed in a special effort to obtain information on relationships between research and development costs and future benefits. Information on the experiences of management in predicting future benefits and in relating realized revenue to earlier research efforts was also sought to supplement similar information obtained through the questionnaires.

Summary of Conclusions

Research and development became a significant activity in a few industrial companies during World War I and has expanded to more companies and increased in amount and significance at an ever-increasing rate since that time. Chapter 2 contains a brief history of the evolution of industrial research and development in the United States and a review of key developments in accounting for research and development costs. The remaining chapters are devoted to discussion of the accounting problems identified in this chapter. The significant conclusions developed in those chapters are summarized in this section.

Definition and Classification. Several approaches to defining research and development are used in practice, most of which attempt to distinguish basic research, applied research, and development. Those distinctions, which are difficult to make in an industrial setting, are neither necessary nor desirable in accounting. The primary need of a definition of research and development in accounting is to provide a uniform basis for classifying expenditures as research and development. Although a general accounting definition of research and development that is precise enough to be used in all companies probably cannot be developed, definitions on an industry-by-industry basis probably can be developed if each industry would establish a committee to undertake the task. By using the criteria discussed and the matrix presented in Chapter 3 of this study, an accountant can help a company to develop a workable and sufficiently precise definition that is consistent with definitions used in other companies.

The distinction between the different kinds of research programs that are found in industry are more significant in accounting than the distinction between types of research and development. Four kinds of programs are found in industry, but only two are necessary for accounting analysis: (1) continuing research and (2) substantial development projects. Differences between the two that have significant implications for accounting are discussed in Chapter 4.

Deferral or Immediate Recognition. Accounting for research and development received little attention in accounting literature before World War I. Early authoritative literature recognized deferral of research and development costs as an acceptable practice, but deferral has not been a widespread practice since research and development became a significant activity in industry. The usual current practice is to recognize research and development costs as expenses as they are incurred.

The theory underlying present generally accepted accounting principles requires that costs be associated with related revenue to measure periodic net income. To accomplish that result, accountants have traditionally divided costs into product costs and period costs and have associated the two types of costs with revenue in significantly different ways. Research and development costs have generally been treated as period costs.

The two-type classification of costs submerges a type of costs with significantly unique characteristics that is identified in this study as "business-preserving costs." Business-preserving costs are discretionary costs and are not related directly to current operations. They are incurred to preserve the profitability of an enterprise over the long term. Research and development costs are a major element of business-preserving costs. Since those costs are intended to benefit the future rather than the present, the theory underlying current practice would seem to require that the costs be deferred and amortized over the future periods that they are intended to benefit.

The requirements of theory, however, are difficult to apply in practice. Costs incurred in continuing research programs should be recognized as expenses immediately. That conclusion represents a practical solution to an accounting dilemma. Immediate recognition is an arbitrary basis of allocation, but alternative methods are equally arbitrary and considerably more difficult to implement uniformly.

Many of the factors pertaining to continuing research also pertain to substantial development projects, but those projects represent a greater concentration of effort, a greater probability of successful exploitation, and a closer link to expected revenue. The need to match the costs of a substantial project with related revenue often overrides other factors. Consequently, the costs of a project should be deferred if they meet the following criteria:

1. A significant project to develop a single product or a series of related products or processes should be established and well defined.

2. The Board of Directors should formally approve the project.

3. Technical feasibility of the products or processes to be developed should be determined and documented.

4. Reasonable probability of meeting planned time schedules for development, production, and sale or use of the products or processes should be demonstrable.

5. The estimated amount and the probable timing of potential revenue should be reasonably established.

6. Only costs incurred after management has evaluated and approved a project should be deferred.

7. Deferred costs should be limited to those that are reasonably allocable to specific future periods or future contracts.

8. A formal program should be established to periodically evaluate the project and to write off the costs that exceed expected revenue less completion and selling costs.

Amortization. One of the criteria for deferring costs is that the costs should be reasonably allocable to specific future periods or contracts at the time of deferral. That criterion provides the recommended basis of amortizing the deferred costs.

Disclosure. Current disclosure practices vary and thus need to be made more uniform. More disclosure is desirable. Generally, a company should disclose the total costs of continuing research for a period as a separate line item deducted from gross profit in its income statement. Essentially the same information, however, may sometimes be disclosed parenthetically in the income statement or in a note to the financial statements. A company should also disclose, if material, the deferred costs of a substantial development project, the amount amortized, and the amount written off as excess costs during the period.

2
Historical Perspective

The history of research and development in the United States since the late nineteenth century divides naturally into three periods with World War I and World War II as the dividing points:

> Early Years (before World War I)
> Middle Years (1914 to 1939)
> Recent Years (after 1939)

Historical factors influenced the growth and expansion of industrial research and development activities in each of those periods and provide useful background to discuss and analyze accounting principles and practices. Evolving principles and practices of accounting for research and development costs more or less paralleled the growth and expansion of industrial research and development activities in the United States.

Early Years

Lone Inventor. Industrial research in the United States in the late nineteenth century was essentially the province of the lone inventor. Inventions of men such as Edison, Westinghouse, Eastman, and Bell provided the foundations for large industries. The laboratories of the lone inventors were in effect extensions of their inventive skills, and research was often based on trial and error methods rather than the application of high-grade scientific and technological knowledge that characterizes industrial research today. Formal scientific investigation was mainly done in university laboratories, which had little direct connection with industry.

The political and economic effects of research and development were not widely understood in this country. Industries based on new inventions tended to start slowly and find their markets gradually; inventions did not cause abrupt and profound economic dislocations.

National Research Laboratories. The United States National Bureau of Standards was established in 1901, giving the country a research center that not only carried out basic research but also became deeply involved in industrial research. The broad pattern for a governmental institution devoted to research had been set in Germany with the establishment of a national physical and technical institute in 1870, shortly after the end of the Franco-Prussian War. The U.S. Bureau of Standards followed that broad pattern. Its functions were to set standards of length, time, mass, and quality, to determine physical constants, to specify standards for materials, and to deal with other matters essential to the nation's commerce.

Company Laboratories. The General Electric Company founded in 1900 the first industrial laboratory in America dedicated to basic research. Two years later the du Pont Company built its "Eastern Laboratory" for research. Other major industrial laboratories organized before World War I were those of Westinghouse, Corning Glass, Eastman Kodak, and United States Rubber. In addition, many companies maintained laboratories as integral parts of their factory operations.

Early Accounting. A search of the accounting literature published before the turn of the century revealed no explicit references on accounting for research and development expenditures. Since the expenditures were relatively insignificant, accounting for them was probably of no particular consequence. References in accounting literature during the early decades of this century were to "experimental expense":

> A ... problem arises in connection with the expenses incurred in making experiments in search of new inventions, now a recognized part of many industrial plants. This may be treated as a part of general expense but there is colorable argument on the other side. An improvement might be secured by purchasing a patent right from an outside inventor. The alternative plan is to hire the inventor to work for the company, in which case the salary and other expenses incurred seem to be the cost of the secured invention just as truly as the price paid for the patent right. If this is so, may not expenses be counted as part of the prospective cost even though the goal has not been quite reached?[1]

---

[1] Henry Rand Hatfield, *Modern Accounting—Its Principles and Some of Its Problems* (New York: D. Appleton and Company, 1909), p. 77. (This comment appeared in essentially the same form in the 1919 and 1927 editions.)

If experiments can reasonably be expected to result in profitable processes, the costs can be charged to capital outlay and the process itself or the patents representing it can be considered an intangible asset. Such a situation is unusual, however, and the proper analysis in such a case seems to be to charge these expenditures to expense; if the experiments result favorably it will be time enough then to revise the analysis.[2]

In 1917, the Federal Reserve Board, after conferring with the Federal Trade Commission and the American Institute of Accountants (now the American Institute of Certified Public Accountants), tentatively endorsed a proposal on approved methods for the preparation of balance sheet statements that contained a section dealing with deferred charges to operations:

> Under this heading, in the balance sheet are grouped such items as . . . experimental charges, etc. After the clerical accuracy of the deferred charges has been verified the auditor should satisfy himself that they are properly carried forward to future operations.
>
> . . . .
>
> (1) The verification of experimental charges carried forward will generally furnish information as to the production and future policy of the company.[3]

The section was approved without substantial change and reissued in 1929—again under the auspices of the Federal Reserve Board.[4]

Accounting authorities had thus raised and discussed the issue of accounting for research and development expenditures before the end of World War I. Significantly, "experimental expense" was being deferred at that time, although the amounts involved and the net results achieved were not of great moment.

Middle Years

The American Association for the Advancement of Science took a major step forward in 1914 by appointing a "Committee of One Hundred" charged with inquiring into the measures that would be necessary to increase scientific research. The appointment of the

---

[2] William A. Paton and Russell A. Stevenson, *Principles of Accounting* (Ann Arbor, Mich.: The Ann Arbor Press, 1917), p. 284.

[3] *Federal Reserve Bulletin,* "Uniform Accounts," April 1, 1917, pp. 277-278.

[4] *Verification of Financial Statements (Revised)* (Washington, D.C.: U.S. Government Printing Office), pp. 13-14.

Committee coincided with the outbreak of war in Europe, and the prevailing neglect of science by most industries in the United States quickly became apparent as the war curtailed imports from Germany, such as dyes, pharmaceuticals, scientific instruments, optical instruments, optical glass, and synthetic organic chemicals.

Germany's scientific and industrial superiority over the United States could be traced largely to the emphasis placed on scientific and technical training. Germany had been granting hundreds of doctorates in science each year whereas graduate scientific training in this country was still in its infancy.

Growth in Research. A tremendous demand for scientists and engineers in industrial laboratories, with a concurrent expansion in scientific training, developed in this country from 1914 to 1939. Personnel employed in industrial laboratories increased from 7,300 in 1920 to 70,000 in 1940.[5] Organized research in the petroleum industry began in 1919 when the Standard Oil Company (New Jersey) created its development department. General Motors Research Corporation was organized under Charles F. Kettering in the following year to continue and to consolidate the research activities which had formerly been carried on in the separate companies brought together to form General Motors Corporation. Bell Telephone Laboratories, which had existed in one form or another since the late nineteenth century, was organized as a separate entity under F. B. Jewett in 1925.

During this period the United States also became the world's unquestioned leader in scientific and technological literature. Through a process of information exchange, fundamental advances largely in university laboratories stimulated development of industrial applications, and those in turn posed new problems for the academic scientist to study.

The conditions under which research and development had to be carried on in smaller factories were often makeshift and less than ideal. As a result, companies often found that a more suitable alternative was to sponsor the research they needed at an established technological research institute. The Mellon Institute, founded in 1913 at the University of Pittsburgh, was the first institute of that type. It carried out a program of industrial fellowships under which the donor

---

[5] H. N. Stephens, "Relations with the Educational System," *Research in Industry, Its Organization and Management*, C. C. Furnas, Editor (New York: D. Van Nostrand, Inc., 1948), Chapter XXVI.

paid the Institute to cover fellowship costs and the "Fellow" devoted his time to the study of the donor's research problem.

Research in several industries was carried out on a cooperative basis in laboratories of trade associations, such as the well-known Underwriters Laboratories and the laboratory of the American Gas Association. In addition, many companies used consulting research organizations of which Arthur D. Little, Inc., established in 1886, is a well-known example.

Although some smaller companies developed their own research laboratories (Merck & Co., Inc., for example), generally only the larger companies in scientifically or technologically oriented industries seemingly could afford to maintain their own separate laboratories. Probably not more than 100 companies had their own research laboratories in the late 1930s, and a rough estimate of industrial research and development expenditures in 1938 was $290,000,000.[6]

Accounting Developments. Accounting for research and development expenditures appears to have been of growing concern during the 1920s to members of the National Association of Cost Accountants (NACA), now the National Association of Accountants (NAA). The NAA discussed the question on at least three occasions—in 1922, in 1924, and in 1926.

W. S. Kemp discussed the subject of "Development Costs and Their Liquidation" at the NAA's first New England Regional Cost Conference in 1922. He stated that "we do not capitalize what might be called research or preliminary experimental work" and went on to say that "all other expense[s] in connection with the development of a product are charged to development account, and that account [is] carried as a deferred asset."[7]

The NAA later queried its members about their handling of experimental expense, and their replies were published in 1924. The following two responses are of particular interest because they distinguish the costs of a continuing research program and the costs of a substantial development project:

> It is perfectly proper to carry [the cost of developing a new article or line] as a deferred account, and an estimate should be made to ascertain the number of units or volume of sale of units,

---

[6] National Industrial Conference Board, Studies in Business Economics, No. 82, *Research and Development: Its Growth and Composition* (New York, 1963), Table 10, p. 39.

[7] *NACA Bulletin*, Volume IV, No. 3, October 15, 1922, pp. 27-28.

as well as an estimate of the length of time over which this development will be spread.

Experimenting [covering the current and ordinary minor experimenting that is continual in most manufacturing establishments] should be charged against current operations each month as the money is expended, and assessed against the lines of products affected.[8]

Two years later one of the participants in an NAA technical session stated that experimental expense should be capitalized "if you are starting out with a new product in which you have very definite knowledge that there is a field for it, and you are going to spend a lot of money and you know it is going to come back to you."[9]

The subject received attention in four noteworthy publications during the middle 1930s: (1) a survey made by Norman B. Clark in 1934, (2) the AICPA's *Examination of Financial Statements* in 1936, (3) the study of Sanders, Hatfield, and Moore, *A Statement of Accounting Principles* in 1938, and (4) an NAA study of 106 companies in 1939.

Clark indicated in his survey, "Accounting for Experimental and Developmental Costs," that, as far as he had been able to ascertain, the extent of uniformity in practice could be stated thus:

Development work on manufacturing methods should be charged to manufacturing expense. . . . [s]ince in most factories, this is proceeding fairly constantly. . . . *work on products already manufactured* . . . should be charged to manufacturing expense and for the same reason.

Development work on new products is quite generally capitalized and amortized over production, or charged off outside of cost.

Fundamental research is generally charged as an administrative expense, or out of surplus, since usually it is not essential to operations.[10]

The American Institute of Certified Public Accountants in its January 1936 bulletin, which was based on the 1917[11] and 1929[12] publications of the Federal Reserve Board, dealt briefly with development

---

[8] *NACA Bulletin*, II, October 1, 1924, pp. 1407-1408.

[9] *NACA Yearbook*, 1926, p. 264.

[10] *NACA Bulletin*, Volume XV, No. 11, Section I, February 1, 1934, pp. 706-707.

[11] *Federal Reserve Bulletin*, "Uniform Accounts."

[12] *Verification of Financial Statements*.

expenditures under the general subject of accounting for deferred charges:

> If development and similar expenditures are deferred, they should be written off over a reasonable period having regard to the character of the expenditures.[13]

The 1938 report of Sanders, Hatfield, and Moore, who had been commissioned in 1935 to make an independent and impartial study of accounting principles, is an authoritative summary of accounting practices at that time. The report noted that experimental expense might be listed in the balance sheet as a deferred charge. It also indicated that allocation rested "wholly upon competent judgment applied to the circumstances of the case" and that "a cautious judgment must scrutinize all charges carried to future periods, to consider whether the benefits anticipated are well enough assured to justify the deferring of the charges."[14]

The NAA made a comprehensive study in 1939 of the accounting treatment of research and development expenditures by 106 companies. The study concluded that the "impression one gets is that there exists a very great reluctance to capitalize research and development expenses."[15] Responses to the NAA questionnaire showed that 87 companies recognized new product costs as expenses as incurred, while only ten deferred the costs. In the same year Stephen Gilman remarked:

> Assigning costs and expenses to the same accounting period in which . . . income is recognized is often impossible due to . . . uncertainty as to time. . . .
>
> Expenditures made for purposes of research illustrate uncertainty as to time.[16]

As more companies faced the problem of reporting substantial expenditures for research and development, a shift away from deferral

---

[13] *Examination of Financial Statements by Independent Public Accountants*, p. 23.

[14] Thomas Henry Sanders, Henry Rand Hatfield, and Underhill Moore, *A Statement of Accounting Principles* (New York: American Institute of [Certified Public] Accountants, 1938), pp. 75-77.

[15] *NACA Bulletin*, Volume XX, No. 13, Section III, March 1, 1939, p. 895.

[16] *Accounting Concepts of Profit* (New York: The Ronald Press Company, 1939), pp. 127-128.

seems to have occurred. Awareness of the problem of uncertainty as to results of research and development expenditures and as to the timing of benefits had evidently become widespread.

Recent Years

America's tooling up to become the "arsenal of democracy" after 1939 wrought a basic change in the attitude of many American industries toward research and development. The scientific and engineering approaches that were used to solve military production problems became a recognized part of industrial activity. Research and development was a completely new function for many companies.

When consumer demand took over from wartime needs after the end of World War II, research and development activity was retained, and the search for new products and processes continued on an ever-increasing scale. Industry had concluded that innovation would lead to higher profits and to greater growth.

Increasing Expenditures by Industry. Expenditures by industry in the United States for research and development have increased at a substantial rate. In the ten years beginning in 1940, they increased fivefold, and by 1960 they had increased to twenty–five times the 1940 level. An estimate of research and development expenditures for 1975 is $21.5 billion.[17]

The industrial sector of the economy accounted for approximately 70% of the nation's research and development effort in 1970; government and institutional laboratories accounted for the remainder. Approximately 44% of the work that companies performed in their facilities was paid for by government agencies. This study is primarily concerned with company-financed research and development (about 56% of the total in 1970) which increased from $2.2 billion in 1953 to $10.1 billion in 1970.[18]

The National Industrial Conference Board estimated the long-term growth trend in overall research and development as being between

---

[17] McGraw-Hill Economics Department, *Business' Plans for Research and Development Expenditures 1972-1975* (New York: McGraw-Hill, May 5, 1972).

[18] National Science Foundation, *Research and Development in Industry, 1970* (Washington, D.C.: U.S. Government Printing Office, September 1972), p. 7.

12% and 15% annually.[19] The report points out that the increase in expenditures for industrial research and development by manufacturing and communications corporations has exceeded growth both in their capital spending and in their supply of capital funds. Thus, the research and development function has become an increasingly important user of company funds.[20]

Increasing Personnel. The National Science Foundation estimated that as of January 1971 the number of scientists and engineers engaged in research and development work full or part time was the equivalent of 359,300 on a full-time basis.[21] That was an increase of 57% in 14 years. Since probably three other persons work with every two scientists or engineers, a reasonable estimate is that about one million persons are now engaged in research and development.

Significantly, the total number of doctorates awarded in the biological and physical sciences and in engineering also increased sharply. A total of 11,283 degrees were awarded in 1970,[22] whereas only 2,000 similar degrees were awarded in 1940.

Effect on the National Economy. The long-term trend of research and development is upward whether measured in terms of expenditure or manpower. That fact has undoubtedly had a quickening effect on the entire national economy. Some portion of the gross national product (GNP) in each year results from the cumulative effect of many years of research. Inasmuch as the rate of growth in GNP in the past decade is higher than the long-term growth rate of the American economy during the first half of this century, a causal relationship between research and development and national economic growth can be assumed.

Postwar Accounting Trend. As the number of companies engaged in research and development increased, competition began to play a more important role in the success or failure of specific research and

---

[19] *Research and Development: Its Growth and Composition, 1963*, p. 20.
[20] *Ibid.*, p. 93.
[21] *Research and Development in Industry, 1970*, p. 10.
[22] National Center for Educational Statistics, *Earned Degrees Conferred: 1969-70—Summary Data* (Washington, D.C.: U.S. Government Printing Office, 1970), pp. 11–13.

development projects. Technological success is now no longer enough to assure commercial success. Discussions with personnel of companies with a long history of research and development indicated that the rapid development of competitive products has reduced the life cycles of products considerably. Increasing competition has increased the uncertainty and undoubtedly has been responsible for an increasing hesitancy to defer research and development costs.

Thomas G. Higgins concluded in a paper presented at the AICPA Annual Meeting in 1954 that "there should be a general presumption that research expenses—whether pure research or general research—should usually be charged off as incurred."[23] He presented the following argument:

> Even though new products may, and frequently do, result from general research, the possibility of the commercial success of any new product at the time of the expenditure is usually so remote that there is no valid basis for deferment.[24]

Mr. Higgins set forth his views on accounting for a development project that may produce a new product affecting future operations.

> If there is reasonable assurance that the [new product] development projects in progress will be commercially successful, there appears to be no reason why the accumulated costs should not be deferred. Should there be any doubt as to this, it seems prudent to charge off the accumulated costs in the current period.
> . . . .
> Development expenses should be deferred only in those cases where they have a reasonable connection with future operations. Their amortization should be over no longer a period than they are expected to benefit and an early charge-off should be encouraged.[25]

The possibility that the accounting treatment of continuing research could be different from that for a substantial development project was recognized again in 1955 by the authors of a textbook:

> . . . the annual cost of operating a research department which is a regular adjunct of the business, and in which the size of staff and scope of activity are fairly stable from period to period, may well

---

[23] "Deferral vs. Charge-Off of Research and Development Costs," *1954 Annual Meeting Papers*, p. 137.
[24] *Ibid.*, p. 125.
[25] *Ibid.*, pp. 126, 137.

be treated as a current expense. . . . On the other hand, wherever research and related costs are incurred in substantial amount on a particular project which is expected to result in a valuable new process, perhaps patentable, there is much to be said for deferring, followed by systematic absorption in later years.[26]

Court Decisions in Tax Cases

Many court cases, mostly relating to taxes during the late 1920s and early 1930s, gave substantial support to the principle of deferring research and development costs. In general, the courts favored deferral. In their view, costs of unsuccessful projects should be recorded as expenses when the projects are abandoned and costs of successful projects should be amortized over the useful lives of the projects.

In most of the cases that were contested, the Internal Revenue Service (IRS) was able to support the claim for deferral. Most cases were not contested, perhaps because they were not material, and the IRS may actually have favored write-off in spite of court decisions to the contrary. For example, Jack R. Miller, formerly a United States Senator from Iowa and a professor of law at Notre Dame, commented in 1948 on an evident divergence between court decisions favoring deferral of research and development costs and the accounting practice of recognizing those costs as expenses as incurred. He stated that deferral of research and development costs "would result in an overstatement of capital more often than their deduction would result in an understatement of income" and added that, in his opinion, the apparent uncertainty about the practice to follow arose from an administrative practice of the IRS.

> . . . that does not appear to square with the [court] decisions. That such practice is in line with business accounting principles simply means that a palliative has been granted . . . [the] uncertainty . . . remains.[27]

Other evidence exists of considerable uncertainty during the early 1950s over the attitude of the IRS toward research and development expenditures. For example, Commissioner Dunlap appeared before

---

[26] William A. Paton and William A. Paton, Jr., *Corporation Accounts and Statements—An Advanced Course* (New York: The Macmillan Company, 1955), p. 312.

[27] "Research and Development Costs," *Seventh Annual Institute on Federal Taxation* (New York: Matthew Bender & Company, 1949), p. 134.

the Joint Committee of Internal Revenue Taxation in 1952 and observed that research and development costs usually are a necessary part of most businesses. He stated that over the long term the effect on corporate income of current deduction of research costs did not appear to differ materially from deferral and subsequent amortization. He also called attention to the difficulties involved in applying specific costs to various projects and processes.[28]

Considerable controversy developed in tax accounting over specific research costs, the determination of lives, and the time of abandonment of a project. The IRS usually allowed research and development costs to be treated as current expenses, and many companies followed that practice.

As expenditures for research and development increased, the development of new products and processes created the need for new facilities, equipment, and working capital. The growing need for capital increased the likelihood that a company would write off research and development costs currently to reduce current taxes. Moreover, considerable pressure developed in scientific and economic circles[29] in favor of immediate write-off for tax purposes based on the belief that research and development costs play an important role in accelerating capital formation and general economic growth.

In light of these developments, Congress in 1954 enacted Section 174 of the Revenue Act that permitted research and development costs to be treated for tax purposes as expenses in the year incurred. Even before 1954 a trend away from deferral was clearly evident in the accounting literature and in accounting and tax practice. The influence of tax practice on accounting practice cannot be determined but the change in the Revenue Act seems in retrospect to have been the final blow to the accounting practice of deferring research and development costs. Although tax procedures should not influence the development of accounting procedures, they seem to have done so.

Survey of Current Practice

The 245 major companies that responded to the AICPA questionnaire were divided into three categories for analysis: (1) durable

---

[28] Commerce Clearing House, *Standard Federal Tax Reporter* (Chicago: CCH, Inc., 1952), Volume 5, p. 6170.
[29] Vannevar Bush, *Science—The Endless Frontier*, a Report to the President, Washington, 1945; John R. Steelman, *Science and Public Policy*, a Report to the President, Volumes I and IV, Washington, 1947.

goods industries, (2) nondurable goods industries, and (3) diversified industries. No significant differences in views were noted between the companies in the three groups. In fact, responses from companies in all three groups were remarkably consistent. The significant findings from the survey are summarized in this section.

Distinguishing Research and Development from Production and Selling. The questionnaire identified eleven functional activities as possible steps in moving a hypothetical new compound from the laboratory to commercial production (pages 80 to 90). The respondents had difficulty classifying the following functional activities: (1) design and construction of pilot plant, (2) pilot production, and (3) using research personnel to help set up initial production runs. The percentage of respondents classifying those activities as manufacturing was almost as large as the sum of the percentages classifying them as research, development, or research and development.

Distinguishing Research from Development. Responses to the questionnaire also indicated that the respondents had difficulty distinguishing research *from* development. The difficulty was evident for two of the activities: (1) searching for product applications and (2) trying to modify the properties of a compound. About 11% classified those activities as research and development without attempting to distinguish research from development. Several of the respondents said that they saw no need to separate research from development, and others said that they had attempted to do so but had found the effort so difficult that they had given up.

Immediate Recognition *vs.* Deferral. The survey showed that the predominant practice was to recognize research and development costs as expenses as they are incurred. Only a few of the respondents deferred research and development costs. About one-half of the respondents said that deferral might sometimes be appropriate for research and development costs of a new-product division of an established company. About two-thirds said that deferral might sometimes be appropriate for the research and development costs of a new company.

Only one-fourth of the respondents indicated that they considered it appropriate for a company to recognize research and development expenditures to maintain its competitive position as expenses currently while at the same time to defer expenditures for expanding its business (page 105). Less than one-half of the respondents considered it appropriate for a company to recognize expenditures for recurring research and development as expenses currently while at the same time to defer extraordinary expenditures on special projects (page 105).

Disclosure. Sixty percent of the respondents informed the public in one way or another of the amounts that they spent annually on research and development (page 108). Of the 83 respondents that did not disclose those amounts, 25 were willing to do so in some manner (page 109). Thus, most of the companies either disclose or are willing to disclose their research and development costs either in the income statement or in some other manner.

The principal reasons advanced by those opposed to disclosure are the problem of establishing a definition for research and development, the danger of giving helpful information to competitors and a belief that, since investors would not understand the significance of the figures, disclosure would be misleading to them.

When the survey was made only a small proportion of the respondents (10%) disclosed the basis of accounting for research and development costs in their financial statements. Although the overwhelming majority did not disclose the basis of accounting for research and development costs, many of the respondents that did not disclose were in favor of disclosure. *APB Opinion No. 22*, "Disclosure of Accounting Policies," issued in April 1972 makes disclosure mandatory.

Classification in the Income Statement. Responses to the questionnaires showed that the practices followed in classifying research and development costs in the income statement were mixed, although most companies deduct the costs from gross profit rather than include them in the cost of sales. Some of the companies identify the costs as research and development in the income statement, but others include them in general and administrative expenses. Some companies allocate the costs to operating divisions and account for them either as part of the cost of sales or as general and administrative expenses. Most companies engaged in research on a large scale have many operating divisions and that may influence the accounting for the costs in the income statement. Costs at the divisional level are more likely to be closely identified with products in the income statement.

Summary

Although early accounting literature and court decisions favored deferral of research and development costs, the historical significance of deferral as an accounting practice is not clear. If deferral was ever predominant practice, practice has certainly changed so that most research and development costs are now recognized as expenses when incurred. Companies that once deferred significant amounts of research and development costs no longer do so. Companies that have long experience with the subject generally defend the current practice as sound and necessary under the competitive conditions in which they operate.

3

Defining Research and Development

The words "research" and "development" are generally used together in industry to describe a distinct function often of independent status similar to production, marketing, and finance. The function covers a wide range of activities that differ from industry to industry. Accountants, businessmen, and most users of financial statements generally view industrial research and development as an activity composed of scientific or technological exploration and experimentation to discover and exploit new technologies, products, or processes or to improve existing ones. The emphasis is on results and the ultimate aim is to sustain or enhance the profitability of an enterprise.

A general consensus on the nature and purpose of industrial research and development, however, has not led to a satisfactory accounting definition that provides criteria to distinguish expenditures for research and development from expenditures for other functions.

This chapter is devoted to problems in defining research and development for accounting as an essential prerequisite to evaluate present and alternative accounting principles for research and development. It begins with a brief discussion of the nature of expenditures that normally are classified as research and development. The discussion provides background for considering the need to define the function and to select distinguishing criteria. An analysis of existing definitions of research and development follows and in turn leads to recommended criteria that companies can apply uniformly and consistently to distinguish research and development costs.

Composition of Research and Development Costs

Research and development costs, like manufacturing costs, can be accumulated and classified into materials, labor, and other costs normally treated as overhead. That type of classification is relatively simple because the nature of expenditures normally treated as research and development, whatever the nature of the research and development activity, are similar in most industries.

Salaries of professional and technical personnel and the cost of related fringe benefits constitute the major element of research and development costs. The National Science Foundation (NSF) found in a 1967 survey that the amounts that industry reported as research and development costs consisted of payroll and related costs, 49%; material, 19%; and other costs, 32%.[1]

Costs of materials and supplies are significant in some research efforts because researchers often need materials that are expensive and difficult to obtain. Also, specifications of high quality standards and precise tolerances often increase the cost of materials. Moreover, some materials considered expendable for research purposes would often be treated as capital equipment if used for other purposes. For example, a research project may require that a car or truck be wrecked or disassembled so that it is no longer usable, and some research equipment may have no other business use.

Other costs consist primarily of depreciation of buildings and equipment, maintenance, and taxes. One common cost is external patent and legal expense including the costs of patent applications and related matters. Costs of liability insurance for clinical studies or product use, fellowships, and profit sharing or other incentives for research personnel are also part of other costs but are usually not material.

Need for an Accounting Definition

Accounting needs to establish precise functional boundaries for research and development. Precise boundaries and cutoff points are also necessary if users of financial statements are to gain a better understanding of the impact of research and development on the financial condition and results of operations of companies. All companies should use the same general principles to determine amounts reported as research and development costs in financial statements because users of financial statements have the right to assume that companies report on a comparable basis.

---

[1] *Research and Development in Industry, 1967* (Washington, D.C.: U.S. Government Printing Office, July 1969), p. 22.

Conflicts in Definitions. Developing criteria that accountants can use to determine expenditures that should be included in and those that should be excluded from research and development is essential because numerous conflicting definitions and bases of identifying components of research and development are used in practice and the term is often used with widely differing connotations. None of the existing definitions appear satisfactory for accounting. Although a scientist or an engineer could readily describe what research and development is, each would likely have a different idea in mind—neither of which would probably be useful in accounting. A satisfactory set of criteria would provide accountants with a reliable means of determining what is and what is not an expenditure for research and development. It would also provide a basis for segregating the costs of those activities of research personnel that should not be treated as research and development and for disclosing research and development costs in financial statements.

Distinguishing Development Costs from Production Costs. Since development shades into production, the problem is partly to distinguish development costs from production costs. Determining a proper cutoff between development and production is difficult in accounting because the two activities often overlap. They often occur concurrently in the same facility, and alternations between them are not unusual. Research personnel often interchange functions with production workers without recognizing the change.

Excluding Technical Support. Companies often classify salaries of research personnel as research and development costs without further analysis. Research personnel, however, may provide technical support to the production and marketing functions as a regular part of their duties. The cost of technical support should be excluded from the cost of research and development and treated as a cost of production or marketing. A clear-cut distinction between research and development and technical support would aid accountants in segregating the costs.

Distinctions between research and development and technical support are difficult to make because the two activities are closely related. A semantic problem increases the difficulty and probably results from the glamour attached to research and development that gives the term "research and development" magnetic qualities. One writer commented that a tendency to upgrade the activities of technical personnel is observable in

> inflation of terms—drafting is called design; design is called development; development is called research and true research is modified for clarity and called "basic research."[2]

By a similar inflation of terms, technical support of production or marketing is upgraded and called "research and development."

Disclosure in Financial Statements. Stockholders and financial analysts want to know more about the extent to which companies are involved in research and development activities, and an increasing number of companies are disclosing information on their research and development activities in published financial reports. Disclosure is often required in registration statements and reports filed with the Securities and Exchange Commission. The Financial Analysts Federation sponsored a study that concluded:

> We believe that it is time for manufacturing companies to report separately the amounts of money spent in each year for research and development.[3]

One writer said that financial executives

> have a responsibility to clarify the role of research and development in their own companies' progress—both in their own minds and in their reports to stockholders.[4]

Existing Definitions

Perhaps the best known definition of research and development is that of the NSF, but numerous other definitions appear in the literature. Also, many companies define research and development in individual ways for internal purposes.

NSF Definitions. The NSF conducts an annual survey to collect data on the total research and development effort in the United States.

---

[2] M. P. O'Brien, "Technological Planning and Misplanning," *Technological Planning on the Corporate Level—Proceedings of a Conference*, James R. Bright, Editor (Cambridge, Mass.: Harvard University Press, 1962), p. 73.

[3] Corliss D. Anderson, *Corporate Reporting for the Professional Investor—What the Financial Analyst Wants to Know* (Auburndale, Mass.: The Financial Analysts Federation, 1962), p. 22.

[4] Edward D. Zinbarg, "Research and Development—The Stockholder's View," *Financial Executive*, July 1965, p. 56.

It defines research and development for that purpose by merely identifying the types of activities that are included and other types of activities that are excluded and requests that companies report their research and development costs on that basis. Thus, research and development

> includes basic and applied research in the sciences and engineering, and the design and development of prototypes and processes. Excluded are routine product testing, market research, sales promotion, sales service, research in the social sciences or psychology, and other nontechnical activities or technical services.[5]

The NSF definition specifies the types of activities that should be identified as research and development and those in turn are defined primarily by specifying the purpose of each type.

Basic research

> includes original investigations for the advancement of scientific knowledge that do not have specific commercial objectives, although such investigations may be in the field of present or potential interest to the reporting company.[6]

Applied research

> includes investigations directed to the discovery of new scientific knowledge that has specific commercial objectives with respect to products or processes . . . applied research differs from . . . basic research chiefly in terms of the objectives of the reporting company.[7]

Development

> includes technical activities of a nonroutine nature concerned with translating research findings or other scientific knowledge into products or processes. Development does not include routine technical services or other activities excluded from . . . research and development.[8]

The NSF definitions of the three types of research and development are used widely by authorities. In fact, most authorities identify the same or minor variations of the three NSF types. For example, the

---

[5] National Science Foundation, *Research and Development in Industry, 1967* (Washington, D.C.: U.S. Government Printing Office, July 1969), Appendix A, p. 87.
[6] *Ibid.*, p. 95.
[7] *Ibid.*
[8] *Ibid.*

Department of Defense uses the same terminology but divides development into three categories—development, testing, and evaluation. A chemical company subdivides development into laboratory, design, and commercial development.

Basic research. Distinguishing basic research from applied research is traditional. Most authorities agree that basic research consists of scientific explorations that are undertaken to expand scientific knowledge in general or the scientific knowledge underlying a particular technology. Other terms used to describe basic research include "pure," "fundamental," and "exploratory." All of the terms imply that the effort is a pursuit of knowledge largely for the sake of knowledge without regard to specific results. That is, basic research is undertaken with the hope that the effort will lead to a fuller understanding of a subject rather than to a practical application of the knowledge gained.

Applied research. Applied research is generally directed to specific practical applications of knowledge obtained from basic research or already available. The objective is to test ideas for new products or processes through experimentation and to determine whether they are technically feasible.

Development. Development generally concerns the practical aspects of bringing a product or process into being so that it can be produced or used commercially. It consists of translating designs or ideas that are technically feasible into commercially exploitable products or processes and may include engineering and testing new products, constructing prototypes, and designing and engineering production facilities.

The terms used by the NSF are sufficiently well known and are sufficiently clear in meaning to be used in this study without further amplification. Other ways of defining research and development are analyzed and contrasted with the NSF definitions in the following sections.

Other Definitions. Over one hundred different definitions of research and development were analyzed during this study to determine why they differed from each other and whether a general purpose single accounting definition could be developed.

Concept of a spectrum. The numerous definitions reflect considerable confusion in semantics, but the concept of a spectrum of research and development underlies many of the meanings. That concept was described as follows:

> At one end of the spectrum is basic scientific research; at the other end, engineering development. Moving from the pure-science end of the spectrum to the engineering end, the goals become more closely defined and more closely tied to the solution of a specific practical problem or the creation of a more practical product. And usually the degree of uncertainty as to the results of a specific project, if successful, decreases as we move across the spectrum.[9]

The concept of a spectrum is based on the implicit assumption that the types of research and development that are commonly identified occur in a definite time sequence. That is, applied research follows basic research and is a necessary prelude to development. The validity of that assumption depends on the observed relationships among the three types of research and development. Basic research, as the name implies, precedes applied research, or rather the output of basic research is converted to practical use through applied research. The scientific principles underlying a technology must usually be found before specific applications can be conceived. Similarly, the research necessary to determine the technical feasibility of an idea for a specific product must usually be completed before engineering and developing production facilities can begin. Alvin Toffler's popular book contains an apt description of the relationship.

> Technological innovation consists of three stages, linked together into a self-reinforcing cycle. First, there is the creative, feasible idea. Second, its practical application. Third, its diffusion through society.[10]

Alternative bases of defining types. Five alternative bases of defining the three types of research and development were identified in the analysis for this study—people, place, purpose, process, and proceeds. The strengths and weaknesses of each alternative are discussed briefly in the following sections.[11]

---

[9] James B. Conant, *Science and Common Sense*, 1951. (Brief reference as paraphrased by Richard R. Nelson, "The Economics of Invention: A Survey of the Literature," *The Journal of Business*, April 1959, p. 105.)

[10] *Future Shock* (New York: Random House, Inc., 1970), p. 27.

[11] Maurice S. Newman discusses the topic more fully in "Accounting for Research and Development Expenditures," *Research Management*, July 1965, pp. 241-260, and "Evaluating Research and Development Activities," *Management Services*, March-April 1966, pp. 24-32.

People. The idea that the types of research and development can be defined usefully on the basis of the training and motivation of the people doing the work is common and depends on an assumed fundamental difference between science and technology. The assumption is that scientists are expected to do research and engineers to do development. Furthermore, if a scientist is motivated by scientific tradition only, his work is considered to be basic research, but if he is motivated by demands of external markets, his work is considered to be applied research.

Training and motivation are clearly factors in assigning personnel to research projects and thus help in identifying the type of work. One suggestion, for example, is as follows:

> The personality requisites of the pure scientist and of the inventor may be quite different, perhaps with those of the applied scientist lying somewhere between . . . . basic research depends on a spirit of free inquiry, which defies planning . . . . scientists should be allowed to follow their research interests and to work with a minimum of restrictions . . . . [development work] differs from basic research in generally requiring more carefully organized teamwork by the many varied groups tackling different phases of the same project.[12]

Since research and development activities consist primarily of the services of scientists, engineers, and other technical personnel, identifying an activity by type of personnel may be useful to management in assigning personnel to projects and in evaluating a research and development program. Another distinction based on people which may be useful in accounting is that a program devoted to research often consists of several one-man projects whereas a program devoted primarily to development usually requires teamwork of many people.

Distinguishing types of research and development on the basis of people is not always reliable, however. The distinction is based on the assumption that technology always follows science, but that is not always true. Research and development in industry varies from highly sophisticated scientific explorations to relatively mundane product development. Many industries require a scientific foundation, but others do not. The drug and chemical industries, for example, require a highly sophisticated scientific effort and employ a large number of scientists, but the heavy machinery and equipment industry has

---

[12] Robert W. Cairns, "The Challenge of Effective Planning for Research," *Chemical and Engineering News,* January 16, 1961, p. 116.

operated effectively with relatively little scientific support. In other industries useful inventions such as "the zipper and the safety razor presuppose little scientific training on the part of the inventor." [13]

Research personnel, both scientists and engineers, often are engaged in production planning, market research, and general troubleshooting without management recognizing the change in function. That tends to undermine an approach to defining types of research and development based solely on type of personnel employed.

Place. The place where research and development activity occurs is often used as a basis to distinguish basic research from applied research and development. The distinction reflects the traditional view that basic research occurs only in the academic environment of a university and that research performed elsewhere must be applied research. The *Encyclopedia Britannica,* for example, distinguishes industrial research from basic research and describes industrial research as essentially applied research and development. The reason for that distinction is evident in comments like:

> The traditions of the scientific community are extremely strong where freedom to pursue research interests is concerned . . . and many of the most outstanding scientists feel that to engage in industrial research would prostitute their heritage.[14]

Place is usually used merely to distinguish industrial research from basic, or what is often called pure research. Basic research seldom occurs in many companies. Nevertheless, the location of research—particularly universities versus industrial companies—is not usually a valid basis for distinguishing types of industrial research and development. Many scientific traditions of universities have been transferred to industry and many large companies carry out basic research. On the other hand, not all research in universities is basic research; many universities conduct applied research that is similar to research in industry.

Another way that place is used as a criterion is to distinguish between the types of research and development performed by large and small companies. Large diversified companies are more likely to en-

---

[13] Richard R. Nelson, "The Economics of Invention: A Survey of the Literature," *The Journal of Business,* April 1959, p. 105.

[14] Richard R. Nelson, "The Link Between Science and Invention," *The Rate and Direction of Inventive Activity,* National Bureau of Economic Research (Princeton, N. J.: Princeton University Press, 1962), pp. 573-574.

gage in basic or applied research because they are better able to exploit unexpected discoveries, whereas smaller companies are more apt to concentrate on improving their existing product lines or to work on new products linked closely to their proven capabilities.[15]

Purpose. Distinguishing the common types of research and development by the purpose of the activity is perhaps the most common basis of defining the components of research and development. Purpose is the primary criterion that the NSF uses to distinguish types of research and development. Basic research is exploring the unknown and contributing to the store of scientific knowledge. Applied research is exploring the practicality of creating or improving products that can be exploited to satisfy unfulfilled needs. Development is creating a reliable product that can be profitably exploited.

Purpose is clearly a factor in management's decision to undertake a research and development program and in budgeting funds for the program. It is also useful in evaluating a program after it is under way. Dr. I. H. Ansoff of Lockheed Electronics Company pointed out that applied research may be justifiable "if it merely holds the promise of substantial improvement in the state of the art," whereas development "is never justifiable unless it holds a promise of making a profit for a company."[16]

Distinguishing types of research and development projects on the basis of purpose may not, however, be useful in accounting. The broad general purpose of a research and development program may be known, but the economic purpose of a specific project, which can be vital in accounting, is not always clearly evident. Basic research projects are designed to serve general goals and cannot be distinguished in terms of their specific economic purposes. The economic purpose of a project becomes more definite after applied research is completed and development is begun, but may be highly conjectural before then.

Process. Some definitions of the components of research and development emphasize the processes involved in the activity. Distinctions

---

[15] W. L. Davidson, "The Case of Advanced Technical Programs," *Management Report No. 69*, American Management Association, 1962, p. 26.
[16] "Valuation of Applied Research in a Business Firm," *Technological Planning on the Corporate Level—Proceedings of a Conference*, James R. Bright, Editor (Cambridge, Mass.: Harvard University Press, 1962), p. 211.

are based on the functions performed, the planning and controls exercised, the amount of resources required, the techniques used, and the degree of success expected.

The techniques are sometimes identified as discovery, invention, and innovation. The process of discovery is described as the "act of wresting a secret from nature," and the process of invention is described as

> purposeful and practical contriving based on existing knowledge (theoretical and applied) and uncommon insight or skill; that is, as the act of bringing to workable conditions a potentially economic or usable process or product that has a significantly novel feature.[17]

Discovery is treated as being in the realm of basic research and invention as being synonymous with applied research. Also, innovation in the sense of introducing products successfully is akin to development. That process is described as carrying on from the point at which value seems probable to the stage of assured production. Thus, in the economic sense of introducing new products successfully, innovation is considered to be the same as development.

Siegel recognized, however, that distinctions based on processes are confusing. For example, the two terms, "discovery" and "invention," are commonly used with an indefinite article—a discovery or an invention—to express the outcome of each process, and in legal and other literature they are often mistakenly treated as equivalent. He also pointed out that while "discovery logically precedes invention, experience indicates that the order is sometimes reversed to the extent that an invention has considerable practical importance. Thus, the invention of all sorts of instruments and apparatus has proved essential to the progress of science."[18]

Proceeds. The proceeds of research or the output at various stages is another basis of distinguishing types of research and development. The underlying assumption is that the tangible results expected from each type of activity differ. Research activity is prompted by the need for information. A researcher is likely to know if he has made a significant discovery that marks the end of basic research and is likely to

---

[17] Irving H. Siegel, "Scientific Discovery and the Rate of Invention," *The Rate and Direction of Inventive Activity,* National Bureau of Economic Research (Princeton, N. J.: Princeton University Press, 1962), p. 442.

[18] *Ibid.,* p. 448.

report the results in a research paper that may be presented to a scientific or engineering group. The technical feasibility of a project has been demonstrated, or the knowledge that a specific device can be built has been gained, and thus, the activity has outgrown the laboratory by the end of the applied research stage. Development leads to a demonstration of the commercial feasibility of a product and a definitive determination of the technical specifications and production requirements.

The proceeds from a successful research project can serve as a measure of whether the project achieved its goals. That type of measurement, however, must be retrospective. Also, unsuccessful projects—projects that did not accomplish the expected results—could not be evaluated on that basis.

Problems in Distinguishing Types

Distinguishing research and development by type creates difficult problems for accounting because basic research, applied research, and development overlap in industry, and precise definitions, boundaries, and cutoff points cannot be agreed on. Each of the alternatives discussed is to some extent arbitrary.

Conflicts in Concepts. Research and development activities do not always conform to the concept of a spectrum because frequently knowledge gained in a later phase may require returning to an earlier phase or one or more phases may be omitted. Distinguishing types on the basis of people is often unsatisfactory because people engaged in research often perform other activities at the same time. Place, in the usual sense, is really not a basis of distinguishing types of industrial research and development, except to distinguish broadly industrial research from research in universities and nonprofit foundations. Using purpose as the basic criterion often fails because the economic purpose of a specific research project is not always evident. Relying solely on technical process distinctions often leads to semantic confusion. Distinguishing types by proceeds or output must await the completion of projects and necessarily excludes unsuccessful projects. Moreover, accidental discovery and unplanned results are often significant in industrial research and development.

Two examples illustrate the difficulties in distinguishing the commonly defined types of research and development in industry–the development of Pyroceram and the discovery of Vitamin B_{12}.

Development of Pyroceram. Corning Glass Works began research on colored photosensitive glass in 1940, starting from previous investigations into methods of producing controlled color patterns in glass.[19] During the experiments a plate of exposed "Fotoform" glass was accidentally heated to 300 degrees centigrade higher than the control setting. The accidental process unexpectedly produced a plate of crystalline material much stronger and harder than originally planned. The properties of the material made it excellent for high-quality electronic circuit boards.

Knowledge thus gained was expanded to develop a general theory about the material, and the project became a team effort directed to two goals: (1) to explore the composition of the material and (2) to develop processes and products. The success of the applied research was disclosed in the company's 1957 annual report.

> ... some 150 business and science writers witnessed the first public demonstration of what may become the most important single achievement in Corning's half-century of organized research—a new family of basic materials which have been given the name of Pyroceram. Pyroceram materials can be made harder than high carbon steel, lighter than aluminum, many times stronger than glass, and resistant to deformation at high temperatures. ... The 8,000 inquiries received since the announcement of these materials indicate the enormous range of their potential use throughout industry.

Product development later resulted not only in cooking utensils now available on the market but also in missile nose cones, ball bearings, ceramic pipe, and other industrial products.

The project began because a scientist had an inquiring nature, and thus, the project clearly is basic research in that aspect. Some argue, however, that research with an economic motive cannot be classified as basic research. Accidental discovery, which is common in many research activities, changed the direction of the project.

The discovery of Pyroceram illustrates another feature of many industrial research and development projects: research may start or branch out for a particular goal but may later branch out to a different goal that produces more spectacular results.

Discovery of Vitamin B_{12}. The development of Cyanocobalamin, better known as Vitamin B_{12}, by scientists of Merck & Co. also illus-

---

[19] S. D. Stookey, "History of Development of Pyroceram," *Research Management,* Autumn 1958, p. 155.

trates the difficulty in distinguishing types of research and development.[20]

After two researchers had discovered that liver contained a substance effective in controlling pernicious anemia, a university scientist reported finding a bacterium that seemed to require something in liver extract as a growth factor. Merck & Co. scientists started from that basic research and tried to isolate the growth factor in liver extract that would be a possible control for pernicious anemia. Since the number of persons suffering from pernicious anemia was not large enough to justify commercial exploitation of the research, the absence of a commercial objective might have identified the activity as basic research. A specific product was involved, however, and the work could have been called applied research even though it was not expected to result in a profitable product.

The result exceeded expectations. The research led to the successful isolation of Vitamin B_{12}, which not only controls pernicious anemia, the original goal, but also has many other important uses. The unexpected discoveries alone may have justified the research in terms of either economic or social benefits.

Business and Accounting Definitions

Business Definition. Some companies find the definitions of the National Science Foundation unsuitable for industrial research. For example, Robert L. Hershey, formerly Vice President and Director of E. I. du Pont de Nemours & Company, pointed out that the NSF types of research and development are not correlated with the various objectives of a business. He believes that, in a business as opposed to a scientific sense, a company must think in terms of research *and* development. Thus, he stated that du Pont classified research into three categories: (1) improvement of established business, (2) exploratory research, and (3) new venture development. Under that system,

> we cannot . . . identify our "basic research" costs, nor our "applied research" costs. But we know very well our costs and their distribution to various broad business purposes.[21]

---

[20] L. Earle Arnow, "A Drug is Born," *Research Management*, January 1962, p. 5.

[21] "Finance and Productivity in Industrial Research and Development," speech delivered at Middle Atlantic Regional Meeting of the American Chemical Society, February 4, 1966.

Some companies undoubtedly must estimate the amounts reported to the NSF as costs of each of the three types of research and development because they do not record research and development costs by types. Some respondents to the questionnaire for this study answered that they could not distinguish research *from* development. Others replied that they distinguish the two but somewhat arbitrarily.

The Industrial Research Institute, a not-for-profit organization that represents the research departments of some 230 industrial companies with large research and development programs, has established a committee to develop a definition of research and development for use in industry. The committee has not completed its work but has concluded that "the common R&D classification schemes are of little help in understanding and generalizing the project selection process."[22] The committee found that the three categories of (1) exploratory research, (2) high-risk business development, and (3) support of existing business are more adequate descriptions of the types of industrial research and development activities than the NSF definitions.

Accounting Definition. The definition of research and development required for accounting purposes is closely allied to the definition needed for business purposes but needs to be more precise. Certain costs should be included, certain costs should be excluded, cutoffs need to be established, and once established, a broad classification of costs may be desirable. Although a general accounting definition of research and development that is precise enough to be used in all companies probably cannot be developed, definitions on an industry-by-industry basis probably can be developed if each industry would establish a committee to undertake the task. Developing an accounting definition that is sufficiently precise for a company is possible. By using the criteria discussed and the matrix presented in this section, an accountant can help a company to develop an operational definition that is consistent with definitions used by other companies.

Costs included. The problem in determining the costs of research and development is generally one of over-inclusion rather than under-inclusion. Too many activities tend to be classified as research and development. The analysis of the various bases of classifying research

---

[22] Robert E. Gee, "A Survey of Current Project Selection Practices," *Research Management*, September 1971, p. 40.

and development by type has been resolved into a matrix showing the characteristics of each type based on people, place, purpose, process, and proceeds.[23] A modified version of the matrix (Exhibit I, page 40) presents some general criteria that accountants can use to assist research managers in industry to determine projects that should be considered research and development and those that should not. Using the criteria would tend to reduce primary research and development costs for many companies, but the addition of costs of other departments for services rendered in support of research and development would tend to increase research and development costs.

Costs excluded. Although the matrix includes technical support because it is closely related to research and development, the cost of technical support should be excluded from research and development costs, regardless of the fact that the work is usually performed by research personnel. The NSF properly excludes from research and development all routine product development, market research, sales promotion, sales services, and similar activities that research personnel often perform in support of production and marketing. Although no reliable statistics are available on the extent of costs of technical support recognized as research and development costs, interviews with personnel of various companies indicated that costs of technical support may comprise a significant portion of amounts that many companies report as research and development costs.

Frequently, research personnel must work with a customer to develop adaptations or formulations of existing products to meet the customer's specifications and requirements. The criteria set forth in the matrix in Exhibit I can be used to assure that the costs of those activities are excluded from research and development costs.

Distinguishing from production. Determining a cutoff between development on the one hand and production on the other is most critical in accounting. The NSF made the following distinction:

> If the primary objective is to make further improvements on the product or process, then the work comes within the definition of research and development. If, on the other hand, the product or

---

[23] Maurice S. Newman, "Accounting for Research and Development Expenditures," *Research Management,* July 1965, pp. 241-260, and "Evaluating Research and Development Activities," *Management Services,* March-April 1966, pp. 24-32.

EXHIBIT I

TYPE OF RESEARCH AND DEVELOPMENT	DISTINGUISHING CRITERIA					
	PEOPLE	PLACE	PURPOSE	PROCESS	PROCEEDS
BASIC RESEARCH Fundamental research Pure research Exploratory research	Creative, curious, unrestrained individuals motivated by scientific tradition.	University or non-profit foundation, government laboratories, and a few industrial laboratories.	To understand the unknown and to contribute to new knowledge.	Investigating new scientific phenomena, discovering secrets of nature, and verifying theories of the physical world.	New knowledge to be presented or distributed to, and evaluated by, a group of scientific peers.
APPLIED RESEARCH Invention Technological research	Creative, curious individuals of varied backgrounds externally directed by market needs.	Industrial, university, government, and commercial research laboratories.	To explore practical possibilities of creating new products and processes. To satisfy heretofore unsatisfied wants.	Creating, inventing or discovering new components, devices, compounds or processes or modifying and combining existing materials, devices, compounds or processes to produce a new application.	Theories or knowledge about natural or industrial materials, processes, and potential products, tests of all areas of uncertainty, and proof of technical feasibility.
DEVELOPMENT New product development New process development Major improvements or new uses Evolutionary inventions Testing Evaluation	Individual effort often reinforced by teams of scientists and engineers, with planning and organizing skills, who work well together.	Industrial laboratories and pilot plants.	To create reliable and satisfactory new or greatly improved products or processes.	Using professional teams with varied skills and greater resources to resolve major technological aspects of new or greatly improved products or processes.	Technical specifications and production requirements for new or greatly improved products or processes.
TECHNICAL SUPPORT Application engineering Cost reduction Product maintenance Product engineering Foreign intelligence Technical information Quality control	Scientists, engineers, and technicians.	Industrial laboratories and production facilities or in the field.	To aid in maximizing the return on current products or product lines.	Using highly trained people and substantial resources to meet varying requirements of the marketing and producing departments.	Technical services or reports as appropriate.

process is substantially "set," and the primary objective is to develop markets or to do preproduction planning, or to get the production process going smoothly, then the work is no longer research and development.[24]

The NSF emphasizes the sequence of the activity as a single criterion. The sequence will not always be useful, however, to make the necessary distinction. Development that is performed by research personnel in central laboratories can easily be distinguished from production. If a major part of development is performed in production units or in the research laboratories of production divisions, distinguishing development from production becomes more difficult.

Production often includes several transitional-type activities, such as production development, market development, and start-up operations, that may easily be confused with development. Production development is an intermediate stage between development and production and is often required for a transition from a fully developed product to a product that can be produced efficiently. If the transitional stage is not recognized, development and production overlap. Start-up operations include starting a production line for a fully developed product. The training of production workers to make or assemble the product efficiently may require extra costs in the learning period.

The mere fact that research personnel perform an activity does not always indicate that the work is research and development. The activity may be in support of production or marketing. On the other hand, production or marketing personnel may perform an activity that should be classified as research and development. If so, the purpose of the activity must clearly serve as a distinguishing criterion.

Frequently, however, other criteria are needed. For example, the expected proceeds from a research activity may sometimes be sufficiently significant to serve as the distinguishing criterion. The technical specifications and production requirements for a new product or process should be clearly drawn at the end of the development period for a particular project. Commercial feasibility is likely to be determined and management generally commits specific funds to proceed beyond the development stage into production.

Subclassifications. The primary accounting purpose of defining research and development is to identify costs that should be reported

---

[24] *Research and Development in Industry, 1967*, Appendix A, p. 87.

as research and development costs and those that should not. Further subclassification should probably be by program and project rather than by types of research and development. Characteristics of research programs are discussed in the next chapter to determine their significance for accounting.

4

Research and Development Programs

Expenditures for industrial research and development may be classified not only according to the commonly identified types (basic research, applied research, and development) but also according to kinds of research and development programs. Research and development programs are examined in this chapter.

Kinds of Programs

Four kinds of programs may be distinguished:
- Continuing research
- Substantial development projects
- New-product development divisions
- Development stage companies

The distinction between programs differs from the distinction between types in that programs are distinguished on the basis of their economic purpose whereas the types of research and development are distinguished on the various bases discussed in Chapter 3. Distinguishing basic research, applied research, and development may be useful to scientists, but the economic purposes of research and development programs have more meaning in accounting.

Continuing Research. Many large companies operate a central research department that works primarily on ideas for new products and on problems not related directly to current manufacturing. Research in those companies is generally organized, financed, and staffed as a relatively permanent operation to provide a company continually with ideas for alternative new products. Scientists, engineers, and other technicians are employed full time to investigate their various scientific areas of interest and to work separately, or in small groups, on many concurrent projects. Although their efforts usually do not affect directly current production, a relatively stable percentage of their projects is expected to be successful and to increase the profitability of the company in the future.

All research personnel of a company with a continuing research program may not work in a central research department. Manufacturing divisions may also have "research" groups whose efforts are coordinated with those of a central research department. Research personnel in manufacturing divisions, however, are usually concerned mainly with improving the present products and processes of manufacturing and are not involved with ideas for new products until development is sufficiently advanced to indicate that a new product can be produced and sold. Work at the divisional level is likely to be directed to product development and often includes technical support of the production and marketing functions.

Substantial Development Projects. A development project that requires substantial resources to carry an idea for a new product through the transition from the laboratory to commercial production may be called a "substantial development project" because it is a concentrated effort with specific objectives. Although projects of that type are not a large part of the total expenditures for research and development in most companies, they are at times material in some companies.

New-Product Development Divisions. Some companies set up a separate division to carry ideas for new products through the transition from the laboratory to commercial production. A division organized for that purpose may be called a "new-product development division." It has essentially the same characteristics as a substantial development project but it also helps established companies to divide managerial responsibility for profit or performance between continuing research, development, and production. A product developed in a new-product division is not assigned to a manufacturing division until it can be manufactured profitably on a large scale. Since a new-product development division is essentially the same as a substantial development project except for the difference in organization, the two may be treated as a single kind of program for accounting.

Development Stage Companies. Although development stage companies are not considered in this study, a brief description completes the discussion of the four kinds of programs. A development stage company is similar to a new-product development division, except that an established company supplies the financing of a new-product development division and a development stage company supplies its own financing. The inherent characteristics of expenditures for research and development in development stage companies and expenditures for substantial development projects in established companies are the same. Accounting for many types of expenditures in development stage companies, however, have traditionally differed from accounting for the same types of expenditures in established companies. In general, accounting for a development stage company stems from the speculative nature of the company and the absence of a cushion of retained earnings to absorb losses and thus sustain the going-concern assumption. Those factors may be more the determinants of accounting for research and development expenditures of development stage companies than the similarity of the expenditures of development stage and established companies.

Refinement for Accounting Analysis

Distinguishing research and development by type and program are two ways of dividing the total research and development activity of an industrial company. Conceptually, each of the four kinds of programs can include all three types of research and development as well as technical support. The diagram on page 46 shows the combinations of type and program that can be found in industry. Although the diagram shows four combinations of type and program, the combinations can be further reduced for accounting analysis. For reasons previously given, new-product development divisions can be combined with substantial development projects and development stage companies are excluded from consideration. Although technical support is usually associated with each kind of program, that activity should be classified as production or marketing, not as research and development. Therefore, the significant classifications for accounting analysis are (1) continuing research and (2) substantial development projects. The features of the two kinds of programs that may affect the choice of accounting methods are examined in the remainder of this chapter.

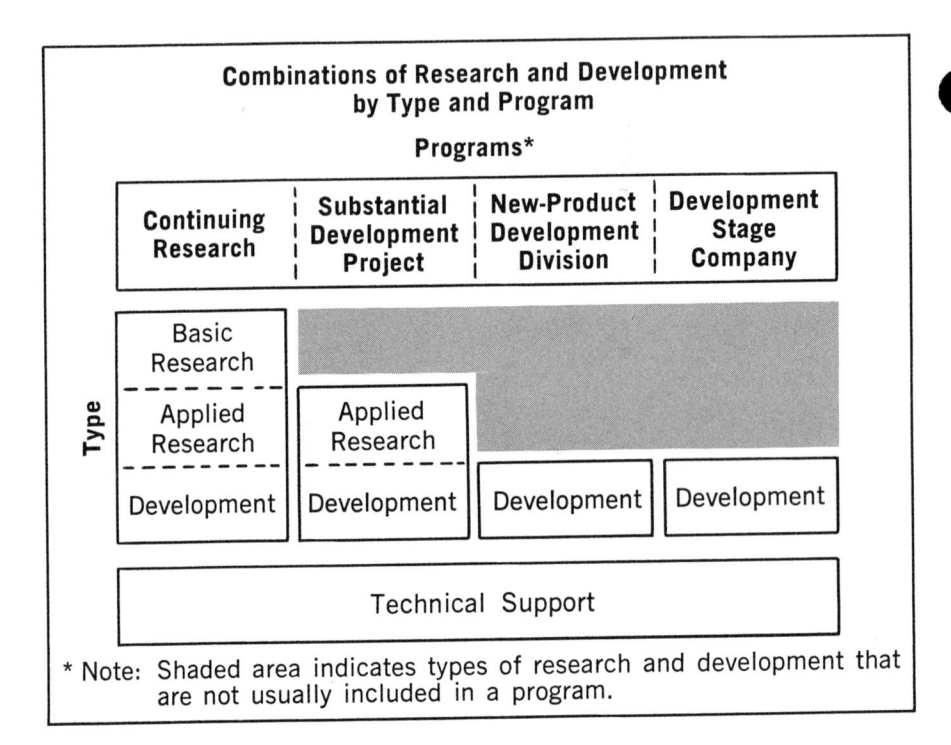

**Combinations of Research and Development
by Type and Program**

Type	Continuing Research	Substantial Development Project	New-Product Development Division	Development Stage Company
	Basic Research			
	Applied Research	Applied Research		
	Development	Development	Development	Development
	Technical Support			

* Note: Shaded area indicates types of research and development that are not usually included in a program.

Features of Continuing Research Programs

The significant features of continuing research programs include the following:

- Composition—preponderantly research with little development
- Concentration in a relatively few large companies
- Personnel costs a major portion of total costs
- Uncertain prospects and long delays
- Relatively stable percentage of successful projects
- Possible correlation between expenditures and sales

Composition. Continuing research consists primarily of basic and applied research with very little product development. Most of the research is applied research, however, since only a few large companies sponsor basic research. Universities and laboratories of nonprofit organizations do most of the basic research in the United States.

Concentration. A small number of large companies do most of the industrial research and development in the United States. Three hundred major manufacturing companies were responsible for 86% of all company-financed research and development expenditures in 1970.[1] The annual research and development expenditures of each of those companies have been estimated at over $2.5 million for 270 companies and $100 million for 30 companies. The steadily increasing dollar volume of industrial research and development expenditures in recent years is traceable primarily to the expansion of existing programs rather than to an increase in the number of companies participating.

Typically, continuing research programs in large companies are organized and administered by specialists. A high proportion of the employees are professional personnel in highly diversified research activities. The programs tend to grow slowly but steadily. Determining the scope of a program is a major policy decision; after the decision, the program cannot readily be turned on and off for short periods.

Personnel Costs. Personnel costs are the major portion of expenditures in continuing research programs. Those costs tend to be relatively stable because highly trained research personnel constitute a scarce resource and are not likely to be released for fear that they cannot readily be replaced when needed later. The supply of skilled manpower, not the availability of projects, determines the projects undertaken. If projects with favorable economic prospects are insufficient, research personnel may be assigned to projects with more uncertain prospects.

Personnel costs for research and development differ from production labor costs in at least one important respect for accounting. Expenditures for production labor almost without exception are assumed to relate to a product that will later generate revenue at least equal to the total expenditures required to produce it. That is not necessarily assumed of expenditures for research personnel. Often, the only tangible evidence of the services received from research personnel is a record of man-hours of scientific effort, the benefits of which are contained in the ideas and observations that may be elicited from notebooks or rough drawings. Therefore the benefits often depend on

---

[1] National Science Foundation, *Research and Development in Industry, 1970* (Washington, D.C.: U.S. Government Printing Office, September 1972).

a company continuing to employ the individuals who observed the facts and developed the ideas. If the entire scientific staff of a company resigned, the company might have little to show for its past expenditures. Even the loss of a researcher by death or resignation might reduce the expected future benefits.

Uncertain Prospects and Delays. A decision to spend money on continuing research represents a discretionary commitment of funds to maintain a competitive position in an industry and to achieve future growth. The decision is necessarily based on a highly subjective evaluation of expected future benefits. Only a slender connection between an expenditure and an ultimate source of revenue may exist when funds are spent. While the expected returns from the overall program may be within a narrow range, the probability of success on a single project may vary from very high to very low.

Knowledge is the only direct product of research and that in turn merely offers an opportunity to proceed further. Many decision points must be passed before full-scale production can be started. At each point, the decision to commit more effort and more funds must be based on the probability of an ultimate profit. Past decisions and past costs have no relevance to those decisions.

Stable Percentage of Successful Projects. The statistical probability of obtaining a reasonable percentage of successful projects is fairly high in a large continuing research program. Two hundred fifteen of the 300 established companies surveyed for this study reported that a relatively stable percentage of their projects were successful. That result reduces the risk and uncertainty of a total research program. Stability can be attributed to the fact that a company is unlikely to embark on a large continuing research program, although willing and able to finance it, without careful planning and systematic procedures for review and evaluation at regular intervals.

Statistical probability of success is enhanced by undertaking many projects at the same time. A one-to-ten ratio of successful projects might mean ten successful projects for a large company with a hundred projects but failure for a small company with less than ten projects. Therefore, even though the probability of success for an individual project is about the same in large and small programs, the ability to undertake more projects increases the likelihood that successful projects will provide funds to continue a program.

Possible Correlation Between Expenditures and Sales. A correlation may exist between (1) long-term growth in sales and (2) expenditures for research and development. The correlation may provide a basis for predicting future sales by periods and determining the effect of current expenditures for research and development on those future sales. Anticipated sales, in turn, may provide a basis for deferring and allocating research and development costs to future periods.

A study in 1968 examined the relationship of research and development to sales for the national economy as a whole and for selected industries.[2] The study was statistical—a ten-variable, multiple regression analysis of sales for the twelve years 1954–1965 on research and development expenditures for the preceding nine years.

The analysis supports somewhat the hypothesis that sales in future periods are increased as a result of current expenditures for research and development. The correlation appears to vary with industry, as might be expected. For example, increased sales in the consumer goods industries seem to correlate with research expenditures several years earlier, but increased sales in the capital goods industries seem to correlate with research expenditures that were made many years earlier. In other words, the consumer goods industries seem to benefit more quickly than the capital goods industries from research expenditures.

The data for the calculations were difficult to obtain and were not sufficiently objective to serve as the basis for general conclusions on accounting for research and development. That type of analysis can be useful, however, in evaluating the overall return on investment in research and development for a company or industry that can develop objective data.

Features of Substantial Development Projects

Substantial development projects share some but not all of the features of continuing research projects. Uncertainty and delay are significant features of both kinds of programs, and personnel costs are the major costs of both. Differences between the two kinds of programs are more significant than their similarities and are discussed

---

[2] Maurice S. Newman, "Equating Return from R&D Expenditures," *Financial Executive*, April 1968, pp. 26-33.

first. The uncertain and variable prospects of recovering costs are then discussed, and finally, a case study of the development of commercial jet aircraft is examined.

Principal Differences. A substantial development project often results from a discovery in a continuing research program and differs from a typical project in a continuing research program in several ways.

- The expenditures required are much larger than for a single project in a continuing research program. Expenditures for projects naturally vary in amount, both absolutely and relatively, but are usually substantial and material to a company.
- More people are involved than in a project in a continuing research program. A large number of people usually work on a single development project, while a continuing research program usually consists of many small projects with one or a few persons working on each.
- Extensive advance design and planning are likely to be completed before a project begins, whereas a project in a continuing research program is usually initiated with little advance planning.
- The likelihood of commercial success is greater and the link to an ultimate source of revenue is closer than for a project in a continuing research program. Management tends to identify expenditures for a substantial development project with the end product and to relate costs to anticipated revenue.

The differences may be sufficient to warrant different accounting. The principal differences significant for accounting consist of larger expenditures, greater concentration of effort, more people, greater tendency to identify costs with expected results, and further stage of advancement in a typical substantial development project as contrasted with a typical project in a continuing research program.

The relative importance of each of the three types of research and development in the two kinds of programs differs. The activities of research personnel assigned to substantial development projects consist primarily of development with little research. The projects seldom include basic research, but applied research is occasionally required to solve problems.

Unlike continuing research programs, substantial development projects are not concentrated in large companies. They may be found in decentralized locations of large companies or in small or relatively new companies and are usually undertaken to develop products or processes that already have at least some promise of commercial success. A substantial development project is usually a single venture with specific objectives and has neither the long-term stability of continuing research nor the possible statistical correlation with future sales.

Prospects of Recovering Costs. The potential economic success of an idea for a new product may appear sufficiently assured at the end of the research stage to warrant incurring substantial additional costs to develop an idea into a product. Although management does not ordinarily incur development costs unless anticipated revenue is ultimately expected to exceed those costs, management has no guarantee of revenue until after the products are both manufactured and sold. A product may appear to be commercially feasible in the development stage, but cannot be produced and sold at a profitable price. Or, a product may be produced at a reasonable cost but may not attract consumers at any price. The nearer a product is to the commercial product stage, the more likely that its future value can be estimated reasonably and the better the determination as to whether its cost will be recovered through future revenue.

Large sums often spent to develop prototypes indicate that management is willing to incur substantial risks in the hope of substantial gains. Past events have proved, however, that large losses may result. Management's hopes for success clearly provide no objective measure of the potential value to be realized from development costs, whether large or small.

Yet development projects are not all alike. At one extreme, success is virtually assured and estimating recovery of cost is not a serious problem—for example, a development project carried out for a customer, such as the federal government, under an arrangement providing for full reimbursement of prescribed research and development expenditures. At the other extreme, significant uncertainty as to whether a project will succeed is a factor in estimating recoverability of its costs. For example, a company may in one fiscal year commit itself to a single, substantial development project and may accept orders even though the product cannot be delivered until the following year. The project may produce substantial revenue in the following year, and the revenue may exceed costs. On the other hand, **the project may fail in the development stage and produce little or no revenue.**

Although uncertainty is a basic characteristic of all research and development programs, the ramifications of uncertainty in a substantial development project are more serious than for continuing research. A period of ten years or more may elapse between the birth of an idea and the creation of a marketable product, and the success or failure of a particular project may not become apparent for several years. Furthermore, the fast pace of invention often makes a product obsolete before or shortly after production begins.

Uncertainty becomes a more significant factor if the success of the company hinges on the profitable completion of a single major project. Some dramatic failures in developing new products have occurred recently. The publicity stemming from those failures tends to overshadow successes. Management, understandably, generally prefers to discount expectations from a substantial project rather than to pyramid expenditures for several years and face the wrath of stockholders if the expenditures later prove worthless.

52 **Case Study—Development of Jet Aircraft.** The development of the first jet airplane for commercial transport by The Boeing Company is an example of a successful development project that involved substantial expenditures and considerable delay and uncertainty before benefits were realized. Boeing began to develop a prototype of the 707 in 1952 but did not complete the first production model until 1957. Although sales began in the following year, the company did not reach a break-even level of sales until 1961. Excerpts from the company's annual reports for the years 1952 through 1961 tell the story succinctly:

1952
The design, development, and manufacture of the prototype (jet transport) will require expenditures estimated to exceed $15 million. These expenditures are being charged to profit and loss as incurred, and are also currently deductible for income tax purposes.

1953
Your company's prototype jet tanker-transport will fly in the Fall of 1954. . . . Expenditures on this project total $12,398,493 by December 31, 1953, and are expected to approximate $15,260,000 at the time of first flight.

1954

In almost every category the prototype jet tanker-transport exceeded estimated performance. . . . The company is hopeful of entering the commercial field, but the decision is dependent on the military requirements and the financial feasibility of such an undertaking. . . .

1955

Ten years ago Boeing first started research on the jet tanker-transport. At that time money was not available either in government or company funds to finance development and construction. It was not until 1952 that the company was in a position to take the financial risk involved in producing a prototype model.

1956

The company's progress and its endeavor to firmly establish itself in the commercial field has been very satisfactory. As of the year end, Boeing had firm orders or letters of intent for a total of 134 commercial jet transports from 11 major airlines.

1957

Total orders for all models of Boeing jet transports stood at 161 at the year end for a commercial backlog of $792 million. . . . Rollout and first flight of the number 1 production 707 ahead of schedule was a highlight of the year. This first aircraft . . . will enter extensive CAA test programs to speed certification of the aircraft. . . .

1958

. . . with developmental and production costs on the commercial jet program exceeding the amounts previously anticipated, a substantial loss is being incurred on the model 707 airplanes delivered or on order. Charges against net earnings applicable to the commercial program totaled approximately $50 million in 1958. . . . Over a period of years it is expected that this commercial jet effort will be rewarding. . . . Charges to earnings to 1958 on the commercial program total approximately $94 million, including the cost of the prototype which was started in 1952. . . . Continuing write-offs of research and developmental, administrative and other general expenses on the model 707 program will have substantial impact on 1959 earnings.

1959

. . . accelerating technological advancement . . . resulted in the cutback . . . of the country's major defense programs in 1959. For Boeing, this meant . . . a reduction in the KC 135 jet transport program. . . . While public acceptance of the Boeing jet transports is enthusiastic and the airlines are highly pleased with the performance and demonstrated earning capabilities of the aircraft, the company has sustained a very substantial loss from the orders received to date. . . . Commercial airplane costs charged to earnings in 1959 totaled $58 million. This amount related to the research, developmental, administrative and other general expenses which were written off during the year and the amount necessary to reduce commercial program inventories at December 31, 1959 to estimated proportionate sales value.

1960

As in the last several years, heavy charges were made against earnings for research, developmental, administrative and other general overhead costs applicable to commercial programs. . . . With respect to the 707-720 programs specifically, fourth quarter book profits exceeded other charges against earnings. Thus, the last impact on earnings of the loss on these programs was recorded in 1960. In 1961 and succeeding years, the 707-720 programs . . . are expected to contribute materially to the annual earnings of the company.

1961

. . . continuation of favorable cost and sales trend on the 707-720 programs resulted in further recovery of prior years' losses on the 707-720 programs.

An executive of The Boeing Company was quoted as saying that the company had at one time been "$160 million in the hole on the first 707 jet and yet 1965 was the best year for profits in the company's history."[3] A concentrated effort to develop a single product or technology may have a significant impact on a company, as the Boeing example shows. Expenditures on the project were sufficiently material to affect reported net income significantly in many years.

---

[3] *The New York Times,* April 15, 1966.

5

Theoretical Considerations

The critical questions in accounting for research and development costs must be evaluated in relation to an accounting system as a whole rather than to existing conventions for research and development. Some of the basic concepts and principles underlying present financial accounting are discussed in this chapter and those relevant to accounting for research and development costs are emphasized.

Present Generally Accepted Accounting Principles

APB Statement 4, "Basic Concepts and Accounting Principles Underlying Financial Statements of Business Enterprises," is the primary source of the description of basic concepts and principles in this study. The historical cost basis of measuring the resources of an enterprise is central to present accounting theory. The past efforts and accomplishments of an enterprise are measured in terms of money expended for resources acquired and money received for resources sold. The measurements are made in conformity with accepted principles of asset and liability valuation and of income measurement. An enterprise initially measures the resources acquired at their acquisition cost and ignores an increase in the value of an asset until a recorded asset is exchanged for money or money equivalents.

The matching concept provides the theoretical basis for measuring periodic net income. Determining net income through a process of "matching" effort (costs) with accomplishments (revenue) conforms to the concept of net income as realized revenue less related costs. The matching concept requires that costs, as far as possible, be associated with related revenue. Conventionally, revenue is recognized and assigned to accounting periods according to the realization principle, although some exceptions are permitted. Costs incurred that relate to revenue of a current period are recognized as expenses; costs incurred that relate to revenue of future periods are deferred.

Concepts and Principles. Six measurement principles now establish the basis to implement accrual accounting and determine broadly the types of events recognized in financial accounting, the basis of measuring those events, the periods in which they are recognized, and the unit in which they are measured:[1] (1) a principle of initial recording, (2) a principle of revenue recognition, (3) three principles of expense recognition, and (4) a unit of measure principle. The principles pertain directly to accounting for research and development costs and are discussed in this section. Since uncertainty and the lack of objective measures often influence the application of accounting principles, the modifying convention of conservatism is also discussed.

Initial Recording. The initial recording principle limits the data that enter the accounting process and specifies a basis of measurement:

> Assets and liabilities generally are initially recorded on the basis of events in which the enterprise acquires resources from other entities or incurs obligations to other entities. The assets and liabilities are measured by the exchange prices at which the transfers take place.[2]

Thus accountants measure assets acquired in exchanges at their acquisition cost, which is retained in the accounts until recognized as an expense according to expense recognition principles. A cost initially recognized as an asset may be allocated to a single accounting period or to several accounting periods in determining net income.

Realization Principle and Cost Allocation. Under present concepts of income determination, patterns of cost allocation are developed in relation to patterns of revenue recognition. The description of the realization principle, the conventional method of recognizing revenue, states:

> Revenue is generally recognized when both of the following conditions are met: (1) the earning process is complete or virtually complete, and (2) an exchange has taken place.[3]

---

[1] AICPA, *Accounting Principles Board Statement No. 4*, "Basic Concepts and Accounting Principles Underlying Financial Statements of Business Enterprises" (New York: AICPA, 1970), par. 144.

[2] *Ibid.*, par. 145.

[3] *Ibid.*, par. 150.

Recognizing revenue on completion of the earning process solves the timing of revenue recognition and revenue thus becomes the controlling factor in the process of income determination. Accountants therefore face the often difficult task of distinguishing the costs associated with revenue of the current period from those associated with revenue of future periods.

Expense Recognition. Expense recognition, the allocation of costs to accounting periods, often proves troublesome. Accountants therefore rely on three expense recognition principles:

>*Associating cause and effect.* Some costs are recognized as expenses on the basis of a presumed direct association with specific revenue.[4]
>
>*Systematic and rational allocation.* In the absence of a direct means of associating cause and effect, some costs are associated with specific accounting periods as expenses on the basis of an attempt to allocate costs in a systematic and rational manner among the periods in which benefits are provided.[5]
>
>*Immediate recognition.* Some costs are associated with the current accounting period as expenses because (1) costs incurred during the period provide no discernible future benefits, (2) costs recorded as assets in prior periods no longer provide discernible benefits or (3) allocating costs either on the basis of association with revenue or among several accounting periods is considered to serve no useful purpose.[6]

Each expense recognition principle represents a different approach; a direct causal relationship between costs and specific revenue is presumed to recognize costs as expenses on the basis of associating cause and effect; the presumption of a direct causal relationship is relaxed in recognizing expenses on the basis of systematic and rational allocation and more or less ignored under the immediate recognition principle.

Product Costs and Period Costs. Generally, costs are most easily associated first with company functions. Functions found in most industrial companies include production, purchasing, physical distribution, marketing, research and development, finance, and administra-

---

[4] *Ibid.*, par. 157.
[5] *Ibid.*, par. 159.
[6] *Ibid.*, par. 160.

tion. The costs of functions must be matched with revenue to determine net income and frequently the basis of association is the relation of the function to a product.

Accountants have traditionally distinguished product costs from period costs in associating functional costs with products and have allocated the two types of costs in significantly different ways. Product costs are associated with revenue by direct identification with specific units of product, whereas period costs are usually associated by identification with accounting periods but sometimes are associated by identification with specific revenue.

Product costs. Traditionally, manufacturing costs—the cost of acquiring and converting raw materials into finished goods—have been identified as product costs in manufacturing enterprises. Product costs are deemed to attach to a product as it passes through the various stages of manufacture. A classic statement of the "attach" notion is:

> . . . the value of any commodity, service, or condition, utilized in production, *passes over into* the object or product for which the original item was expended and *attaches to* the result, giving it its value.[7]

Product costs consist of costs generally associated with readying a product for the market, including labor and materials consumed in manufacturing the product, indirect manufacturing costs, and administrative costs closely allied to manufacturing. Costs, such as direct labor and direct materials, that tend to vary with output are assigned to specific products. Costs that are difficult to assign specifically, or that tend to be fixed because they vary more with time than output, are classified as indirect product costs. Accumulated indirect costs are assigned to products on various systematic and rational bases of allocation. Assigned costs remain classified as assets until the enterprise sells the products. Product costs are thus recognized as expenses on the basis of associating cause and effect, and the "costs attach" notion provides the rationale for the presumed causal relation with specific revenue.

Period costs. Costs that are not treated as product costs have been referred to traditionally as period costs. Typically, they include the costs of selling, advertising, distributing, research and development,

---

[7] William A. Paton, *Accounting Theory* (New York: The Ronald Press Company, 1922), pp. 490-491.

and general administration. The term period costs is used in this study in the sense of its usual meaning, although it is sometimes used in accounting literature to mean costs that are recognized as expenses as they are incurred. Period costs must also be associated with related revenue to measure net income. They may in principle be allocated to (1) a future period or periods, (2) the current period, (3) a past period or periods, or (4) a combination of past, current, and future periods.

Deferring period costs is consistent with the expense recognition principle of associating cause and effect if future benefits are (1) known or (2) expected with reasonable certainty or (3) the purpose of the expenditure was to secure future benefits. The first condition never exists since the future is always uncertain. Accountants rarely consider the third condition. Thus the present practice is to defer period costs only if future benefits can be expected with reasonable certainty. Period costs that are deferred often include expenditures for patents, copyrights, advertising, organization costs, and research and development.

A period cost is recognized as an expense in the period in which it is incurred on the basis of associating cause and effect if a direct or indirect association with that period and with no future period is presumed. For example, the estimated cost of warranty expense and expenditures for sales commissions and delivery expenses are recognized on that basis. A period cost may be recognized as an expense in the period in which it is incurred on the basis of systematic and rational allocation if it benefits only the current period. Other period costs may be recognized as expenses in the period in which they are incurred because they provide no discernible benefits to any period or because associating them with revenue or allocating them among several periods is considered to serve no useful purpose.

Conservatism. The modifying convention of conservatism often overrides the basic principles of associating costs with revenue. Business enterprises operate under conditions of uncertainty, and accountants are often reluctant to recognize expenditures as assets without some objective evidence of future benefits or some reliable method of determining value. Therefore companies often classify costs as current expenses even though the costs can be reasonably expected to benefit future periods. The practice demonstrates an unwillingness to attribute value to an effort with a high degree of uncertainty as to future benefits.

Summary of General Theory. The principles of initial recording, revenue recognition, and expense recognition provide the theoretical basis for measuring income and for solving the cost allocation problem under the present historical cost basis of accounting. Accountants traditionally divide costs into product costs and period costs, and associate the two types of costs with revenue in different ways. Since revenue is assigned to periods first usually in conformity with the realization principle, costs that are expected to produce revenue or other benefits in future periods should be deferred and associated with the revenue of those periods if the benefits are reasonably certain to be realized. Thus, the present theory of income measurement provides a strong argument for deferring research and development costs until expected revenue is realized.

Practical Problems

The critical problems in accounting for research and development costs stem from the need for periodic financial statements. Determining net income requires many complicated measurements, decisions, and allocations, including the use of properties, accrual of liabilities, realization of revenue, and allocation of costs to specific periods. Accounting for research and development costs involves many of the same types of decisions as accounting for other costs, but the answers may justifiably differ and practical problems may override theory because some characteristics of research and development are unique.

The general method of associating costs with revenue may be modified for practical reasons in many circumstances. For example, the average lives of many attachments and components are less than one period, and the costs of the items are normally treated as expenses of the period in which the items are acquired even though they may not be consumed entirely in that period. Likewise, costs of rebuilding production equipment are usually treated as current expenses because predicting the extended useful life of the equipment is often impractical. Costs of production equipment of low unit value and items in common use—such as nuts, bolts, screws, and washers—are often recognized as expenses in the period when purchased rather than in the period consumed.

Associating Costs with Revenue. Research and development costs are incurred to acquire economic resources that should be recognized initially as intangible assets in accordance with the theory underlying present accounting. Determining a reasonable and defensible basis of allocating the costs of the assets to implement the theory is ordinarily a major problem. Implementation is often difficult because the benefits, if any, may be realized long after the costs are incurred and some benefits are widely scattered. Even with hindsight, relating specific costs of research and development with specific benefits is often impossible. Since benefits expected from research and development often cannot be associated with specific products or specific periods, accountants generally reject an attempt to associate costs of research and development with related benefits. The survey conducted for this study confirms that most companies recognize research and development costs as current expenses (see Appendix).

The alternative of deferring research and development costs and allocating the costs on a systematic and rational basis is used sparingly and for diverse and sometimes conflicting reasons. Since no uniform criteria have been established to guide the selection of procedures, one company may defer and amortize research and development costs and another in apparently similar circumstances may record similar costs as current expenses. Paradoxically, a development stage company whose sole activity may consist of a single substantial development project often defers all research and development costs while an established company recognizes similar costs as current expenses.

Classifying as Product or Period Costs. Distinguishing costs that can be associated with specific products and those that cannot is necessary to implement the "costs attach" notion in manufacturing enterprises. Distinguishing product costs from period costs provides little help, however, in answering two critical questions in accounting for research and development costs: (1) what portion of research and development costs should be deferred? and (2) to what periods should deferred costs be allocated?

Business-Preserving Costs

An alternative three-way classification of costs may prove more useful in associating research and development costs with revenue than the distinction of product or period costs. Treating all nonmanufacturing costs as period costs conceals important differences between the various components.

A component of period costs with unique characteristics that has become increasingly significant during the last several decades can generally be described as "business-preserving costs." Recognizing that component of period costs as a separate category could ultimately improve accounting for those costs. Business-preserving costs are the numerous discretionary expenditures that are not required for the current production and marketing efforts but that aim to maintain the enterprise in the future. The costs, which are regular and recurring in many companies, include institutional advertising, executive development, long-range planning, medical examinations of key employees, mineral exploration, research, and development of new products.

Some business-preserving costs are for protection; examples are medical examinations to preserve the health of employees and research programs to preserve the vitality of the company. Other costs relate to prevention; examples are safety programs to prevent employee accidents and maintenance programs to keep machinery and equipment in good running order. The major part of business-preserving costs, however, is to maintain and enhance the long-range earning capacity of the enterprise; for example, executive development, supervisory training, institutional advertising, and most research and development.

Necessary Costs. To remain profitable, a business enterprise must constantly update its products by developing new competitive products or technologies. To be able to select new products or technologies that are competitive, however, an enterprise must be able to choose from alternatives, which are rarely available at no cost and are usually the result of a painstaking, deliberate, and costly effort in a continuing research program.

The availability of promising alternatives, of course, does not in itself insure that the products chosen will be competitive. Success requires coordinating highly developed resources. Executives and staff must be trained and plans for production and distribution must be efficient.

Optional Timing of Costs. Business-preserving costs are discretionary in the sense that they do not need to be incurred during a particular period if management chooses to eliminate them, but management cannot postpone incurring the costs for long without jeopardizing the competitive position of the enterprise. Management justifies incurring the costs on the grounds that revenue of future periods will increase or at least remain at current levels, not on the grounds that current revenue will increase.

Associating Business-Preserving Costs with Revenue

Since business-preserving costs usually cannot be related directly to specific products, associating the costs with related benefits is difficult. Most companies now deduct business-preserving costs from revenue in the period in which the costs are incurred, conforming to the immediate recognition principle. Since the bulk of business-preserving costs is incurred to provide future benefits, the reason for recognizing the costs as expenses as incurred must be that attempting to associate them with future revenue or future accounting periods is considered to serve no useful purpose. Often the reasons are that the costs are regular and recurring, the amount relating to future periods is immaterial, and no logical basis of allocating the costs to future periods can be found.

Objection to Present Practice. The weakness of present accounting for business-preserving costs is evident. Since the costs are unrelated to current revenue, the presumption must be that management believes that the costs benefit some future period or periods. The increase in number, size, and activity of research divisions of major companies, for example, presupposes satisfaction with research performance and reflects a belief that research is creating value in the form of future revenue or future savings in costs.

Deferring Business-Preserving Costs. An alternative to the predominant current practice would be to defer and allocate business-preserving costs on some reasonable basis.

Arguments for deferral. An argument can be made that business-preserving costs should be deferred and allocated to future years by either (1) relating the costs to future products and associating them with the revenue from the sale of those products or (2) relating and allocating the costs to future periods in which benefits are expected.

Deducting business-preserving costs as expenses currently may affect net income significantly in some periods. For example, a company with unsatisfactory current earnings may spend large sums on marketing and advertising to increase revenue in future years. Under current practice, the expenditures are usually deducted from revenue of the current period, not from revenue of the future periods expected to benefit from the expenditures.

Frequently, business-preserving costs relate to development of an entirely new activity, diversification of products, or relocation or expansion of an existing activity. The costs are likely to be recorded as assets if the requisite knowledge, experience, or regional franchises are acquired through the acquisition of a business. Similar costs are usually recorded as expenses immediately if the requisite resources are developed internally by staff personnel or consultants.

Arguments against deferral. A plausible argument is that although business-preserving costs are discretionary and pertain to the future, they are necessary to preserve the current level of operations of an enterprise. The argument holds that an enterprise should recognize as current expenses all costs necessary to preserve its capacity to operate competitively in an ever-changing economic environment. Thus, business-preserving costs should be recognized as expenses in the period incurred to the extent that they are necessary to preserve the enterprise.

Arbitrary deferral. An intermediate step between recognizing the costs as expenses immediately and deferral and allocation based on association with benefit would be deferral and allocation over a selected period, say five years.

Implications of Concept. The concept of business-preserving costs is a useful analytical tool in evaluating present and alternative accounting for discretionary costs, such as research and development costs. An enterprise could produce the same number of products in the current period whether or not it incurred business-preserving costs. The favorable effect of the expenditures on products, revenue, or net income is over the long term. Thus, business-preserving costs benefit the future more than the present but their effects on specific future products or specific future periods cannot usually be identified. The expenditures usually create resources, even though their value is uncertain, but the argument for deferring the costs is difficult to support because no direct relationship to specific future revenue either by products or accounting periods can be demonstrated.

The argument that business-preserving costs should be recognized as expenses immediately contains an obvious flaw in that it introduces criteria for associating cost with revenue that are difficult, if not impossible, to justify in theory. Determining the costs necessary to preserve an enterprise is probably impossible because the negative effects of not incurring costs, like the positive effects of incurring them, become evident only over the long term. Many discretionary costs clearly go beyond sustaining the current level of operations of an enterprise. Highly organized marketing programs may encompass several years; entering new markets may entail substantial promotion costs that have little or no relation to products sold currently.

Discretionary costs, which are described in this study as business-preserving costs, need further study before the concept can be applied to develop accounting recommendations under the present basis of accounting. The various types of discretionary costs need to be studied separately to determine whether the costs should be deferred. That most business-preserving costs are now accounted for as period costs does not imply that all business-preserving costs should be recognized as expenses as incurred.

6

Recommended Accounting

The present historical cost basis of financial accounting has been attacked increasingly, both from within the accounting profession and from without. Some critics call for a basic change in financial accounting, by conversion to current value accounting, for example. Others believe that present accounting is basically sound but that the accepted alternative methods in various areas, including accounting for research and development, should be reduced. This study endorses restrictions on alternatives; it does not attempt to restructure present financial accounting.

The decisions to be made in this chapter are to determine (1) the extent to which the present predominant practice of recognizing research and development costs as expenses as incurred should be continued and made uniform, (2) the extent to which these costs should be deferred and allocated to future periods or specific products, and (3) the period and basis of amortization of the deferred costs. Since the characteristics of the two types of research and development programs discussed in Chapter 4—continuing research and substantial development projects—differ, the two types of programs are discussed separately.

Continuing Research

A continuing research program consists primarily of basic and applied research projects, although it often includes some minor development projects. Management budgets funds for the program not only to preserve a level of income but also to create a higher level, in the belief that the expenditures will produce future benefits in the form of new product sales and profits. Costs that produce future benefits create assets and should in theory be deferred and allocated to future revenue. In practice, however, the costs of a continuing research program are usually recognized as expenses as incurred.

Deferral or Immediate Recognition. Since most of the costs of a continuing research program are business-preserving costs, deferring and allocating the costs on some systematic and rational basis over the periods of expected benefits seems to be justifiable in principle. The crucial question, however, is how to justify deferral if a direct relationship to specific future revenue, either to products or to periods, cannot be demonstrated.

As indicated in Chapter 4, a recent study[1] suggests the possibility of a causal relationship between costs of basic and applied research—the predominant activities in continuing research programs—and increases in revenue in later periods. The findings, however, were inconclusive. A causal relationship between specific costs of research and specific revenue in future periods simply cannot be demonstrated for most companies, even with the benefit of hindsight.

Research pertains to the new and untried, and a company engaging in research is uncertain about the benefits that may be realized from its efforts. Even though a research project may reasonably be expected to be successful, the amount and timing of benefits are uncertain. If a project is successful, the duration and value of the benefits are uncertain.

A company may sometimes be able to determine in retrospect, although not easily, that certain revenue was made possible by certain expenditures for basic or applied research, but it is never able to look into the future and determine that specific current expenditures for research will be the source of future revenue.

Moreover, the purpose of research is to develop ideas for new products generally and the costs cannot usually be associated with specific products. The activities in a continuing research program usually consist of numerous projects in various stages. To measure the cost of individual projects under those circumstances would require the allocation of joint costs, and the possibility of developing a satisfactory basis of allocation is not promising.

---

[1] Maurice S. Newman, "Equating Return From R&D Expenditures," *Financial Executive*, April 1968, pp. 26-33.

The survey conducted for this study indicates that many research projects are unsuccessful (see Appendix). A large percentage of the costs of a continuing research program in many companies, therefore, produces no specific benefits in future periods. Some accountants may argue that the total cost of the research effort should be deferred and matched with the benefits from successful projects. That argument, however, is difficult to sustain. A company has a known loss to the extent of the cost of an unsuccessful research project. Deferring known losses would burden future periods with costs that provide no benefits.

The costs of a continuing research program tend to be fairly stable from year to year, and the percentage of total costs that relate to successful research projects is often immaterial, even though the value of a successful project may be substantial. The periodic costs of all projects in a continuing research program would normally tend to be about the same as the amount amortized each period under most conceivable methods of deferral and amortization. Thus, after an initial start-up period, the amount recognized as expenses in a period would tend to be about the same under most allocation methods, including immediate recognition.

Conclusion for Continuing Research. Although sound theoretical reasons can be marshalled for deferring at least some portion of the costs of continuing research programs and for allocating those costs over the periods of expected benefit, the characteristics of continuing research programs invalidate most possible methods.

A causal relationship between specific costs of research and specific future revenue, either by products or by periods, cannot be readily developed and applied. Benefits from basic or applied research projects are usually uncertain and, even if reasonably assured, are diffused and unquantifiable. Many companies abandon a large percentage of their research projects because the projects are unsuccessful and provide no future benefit. Many costs are joint costs and a reasonable basis of allocation to specific products or processes cannot be developed.

All costs of continuing research programs should therefore be recognized as expenses at the time incurred. The conclusion is primarily practical. Recognizing costs immediately as expenses is admittedly an arbitrary allocation of costs, but other methods of allocation are equally arbitrary and considerably more difficult to implement uniformly. The recommended method of accounting for costs of a continuing research program will achieve uniformity and is unlikely to cause substantial fluctuations between periods because the costs of most programs are relatively stable.

Substantial Development Projects

A substantial development project represents a concerted effort to develop new products or processes that have already proved to be technically feasible. Costs of a project have many similarities to costs of a continuing research program. Therefore, many of the factors related to business-preserving costs and a continuing research program apply to a substantial development project. The distinguishing characteristics of a substantial development project may, however, be sufficiently unique to warrant different accounting. Significantly, a substantial development project represents a greater concentration of effort, has a greater likelihood of success, and has a closer link to an ultimate source of revenue than projects in a continuing research program.

Uncertainty. Deferring the cost of a substantial development project, like deferring the cost of a continuing research program, would introduce in the balance sheet costs that may never be recovered. Many projects are unsuccessful and obviously produce little future benefits. Distinguishing a successful project from an unsuccessful one is often difficult because even promising projects may become worthless before potential benefits are realized. A company may be forced to abandon a promising project if, for example, a competitor reaches the market first with a product that is as good or better. Since many duplications of effort occur in industrial laboratories, that possibility may occur many times.[2]

Inability to Determine Recoverability of Costs. Since future benefits are uncertain, the recoverability of the costs of a substantial development project cannot be determined objectively. Determining the recoverability of costs is difficult and necessarily subjective because it must be based on informed opinions—even those best qualified to

---

[2] James A. McFadden pointed out in "New Concepts of Information for Decisions—Research and Development" that no company can do more than 2% of the total research done in the United States so that 98% represents intellectual and materialistic competition. *NAA Bulletin,* August 1959, Sec. 3, p. 25.

evaluate a project must base their evaluations on subjective opinions. Those closely associated with a substantial development project are rarely able to predict the eventual outcome with a reasonably high level of confidence.

Determining the recoverability of the costs of a project is particularly troublesome if development is mixed with production, which occurs, for example, in developing a new airplane or missile. The design and engineering knowledge gained from building a prototype are valuable, but whether expected revenue will equal or exceed the costs is difficult or impossible to foresee. The influence of conservatism is strong and accountants may be reluctant to defer costs of projects if recovery of the costs is not reasonably certain. The costs unlikely to be recovered are potential losses that should probably be recorded as current expenses.

Need to Defer. The need for objective criteria for valuation and the influence of conservatism are often outweighed by the greater need to match significant costs of substantial development projects with expected revenue in later periods. The greater the certainty that a project will contribute to the future earnings of a company, the greater the need to defer the costs incurred. Thus a company may be justified in deferring the costs of one project and recording the costs of another as current expenses. The crucial question is whether workable criteria can be established to resolve the quandary in deciding which costs should be deferred.

Criteria for Deferral. Criteria are necessary to make operational a selective basis of deferral. A review of the circumstances surrounding substantial development projects, both successes and failures, indicates that certain information about the projects is known or could be discovered at or near the outset of a project. Available evidence also indicates a degree of correlation between unsuccessful projects and the lack of information on certain key points. Information on those key points can provide the basis for criteria that a project should meet if the costs are to be deferred. Recommended criteria are that:

- A significant project to develop a single product or a series of related products or processes should be developed and well defined.
- The Board of Directors should formally approve the project.
- Technical feasibility of the products or processes to be developed should be determined and documented.

- Reasonable probability of meeting planned time schedules for development, production, and sale or use of the products or processes should be demonstrable.
- The estimated amount and the probable timing of potential revenue should be reasonably established.
- Only costs incurred after management has evaluated and approved a project should be deferred.
- Deferred costs should be limited to those that are reasonably allocable to specific future periods or future contracts.
- A formal program should be established to periodically evaluate the project and to write off the costs that exceed expected revenue less completion and selling costs.

Those criteria can be used to identify a substantial development project and to determine costs that should be deferred. The criteria are discussed in the remainder of this section.

Identifying a substantial development project. Identifying a substantial development project is largely a matter of judgment. The size of the financial commitment, its relative significance to the company, and the existence of well-defined products or processes in the development stage are factors that should be considered. A project is clearly significant if its success or failure would have a material financial effect on the earnings of a company. A series of closely related lesser projects which are significant in total may have the same potential economic effect on a company as a single significant project.

Committing a substantial amount of funds that exceeds the amount normally spent on a continuing research program would also indicate a substantial development project. Funds committed should exceed significantly the amount determined by projecting the trend of the past costs of a continuing research program. For example, the employment of additional scientists and engineers specifically for the project would be objective evidence that a company had made a significant commitment to a substantial development project.

Formal approval. Formal approval by the Board of Directors would assure that the project had been approved at the highest policy level. Management directors would need to justify the project to outside directors who should be able to appraise the project objectively.

Technical feasibility. Accountants are generally not qualified to appraise the technical feasibility of a development project and usually must rely on opinions of the scientific personnel assigned to the project. Frequently, the existence of pilot models may provide objective evidence that the desired technical result can be achieved. An example is the so-called "breadboard" model of electronic computers: all that is required to achieve large-scale production is money, time, and talent.

Employing outside consultants to appraise technical feasibility presents a problem because companies must usually maintain secrecy for competitive reasons. Further, finding individuals outside of a company who have the necessary background and skills to make a competent evaluation is often difficult.[3]

Timing. Deferring costs of substantial development projects would tend to substitute one arbitrary procedure for another unless the expected timing of development, production, and eventual sale or use of the product to be developed is reasonably determinable. For example, writing off costs over five years without evidence that five years is the period of expected revenue may be as arbitrary as immediate write-off. Many companies, however, adopt and adhere to schedules within reasonable limits. For example, a critical path schedule or some equivalent is partial evidence of reasonable probability as to timing. Other evidence of that type could also support an authorization to defer costs.

Reasonable probability of revenue. A high probability of future revenue should be evident before costs of a substantial development project are deferred. Revenue is more or less guaranteed for some types of projects. The most obvious example is a project conducted under a contract that requires satisfactory performance only. A less obvious example of a project with a reasonable probability of revenue is one to develop a product that reputable customers are committed in advance to buy or lease. A typical arrangement is often found in the computer industry, but many large or complex industrial machines of a specialized nature are developed under similar arrangements. The selling price and estimated costs are often closely related, and the buyer is often willing to assure or protect the seller to obtain the equipment. If revenue is not guaranteed or fairly evident, deferring

---

[3] Edward B. Roberts, "How the U.S. Buys Research," *International Science & Technology Digest,* September 1964, p. 74; also Paul W. Cherington, Merton J. Peck, and Frederick M. Scherer, "Organization and Research and Development Decision Making within a Government Department," *The Rate and Direction of Inventive Activity,* National Bureau of Economic Research (Princeton, N. J.: Princeton University Press, 1962), pp. 402-405.

- costs should be supported by other presumptive indications of the reasonable probability of revenue.

Applicable costs. Before a company decides to embark on a substantial development project, some evidence should be available that management has assessed the risk, understands the profit potential, and has estimated reliably the costs to be incurred. Those procedures probably indicate that the first five criteria of significance, formal approval, technical feasibility, timing, and reasonable probability of revenue are met.

After the decision to defer costs has been approved, all direct costs and a reasonable allocation of overhead costs incurred on a project should be deferred. Prior costs of research that might have contributed to the project should not be deferred retroactively. Costs of a continuing research program that might be allocable to a substantial development project would have been incurred regardless of the project and should not be allocated to the project.

Specific deferral. Costs allocable to a project should be reasonably allocable to specific accounting periods or future contracts in relation to the projected revenue. In other words, deferred costs that appear in a balance sheet should generally be allocable to the specific time periods or products to which they relate. If the information needed for that designation is unavailable, a possible conclusion is that costs of the project are not specifically related to a particular product or process and should not be deferred.

Excess costs. Allocable costs may exceed the expected revenue even though a project may meet all other criteria. Costs and expected revenue of a substantial development project are likely to be more closely related than for projects in a continuing research program, but the costs may increase rapidly and beyond estimates if a company is forced to meet deadlines. If current estimates of the costs required to complete and sell a product exceed the expected revenue, the excess should be written off immediately as losses. Thereafter, expected revenue and expected costs should be analyzed periodically—at least quarterly, if interim statements are published quarterly—and excess costs should be written off.

- **Amortization of Deferred Costs.** The amounts of the deferred costs of a substantial development project that are amortized should be deducted from the revenue of the periods benefited. One criteria for deferral is that only those costs that are allocable to specific future periods should be deferred. That criteria provides a basis for allocating the costs to time periods. Specific deferral requires that costs be reasonably allocable to specific periods or future contracts at the time deferred. That requires estimates of the amount and timing of future revenue and provides a systematic basis for allocation. Although estimating the total amount of revenue expected from a given expenditure is admittedly difficult, accountants face and solve the same kind of problem for a depreciable asset. Estimates of the lives of fixed assets are often inaccurate; many assets are in use long after they are fully depreciated or assets are abandoned before they are fully depreciated. Since uncertainty is the essence of the future, all that can be reasonably expected is that accountants make the best estimates possible at the time of deferral.

Conclusions for Substantial Development Projects. The need to match the cost of a substantial development project with related revenue overrides other considerations if material costs are incurred on a project that has a reasonable probability of success and a high likelihood of future benefits. Criteria have been developed in this chapter to distinguish projects that qualify for deferral from those that do not. Costs of projects that comply substantially with all of the recommended criteria should be deferred and allocated to future revenue. Projects that meet the criteria are not expected to be numerous in any one company. The costs of relatively minor development projects should be recognized as current expenses in the same way as the costs of continuing research programs.

Disclosure in Financial Statements

Some companies now include information in their annual reports or in press releases on their research and development costs. Financial analysts and other users of financial statements urge more consistent disclosure of that type of information in financial statements. Many users insist that a company should disclose research and development costs separately in the income statement and disclose its accounting policies for research and development costs. The demands of users of financial statements for more consistent disclosure appear reasonable.

Continuing Research. Expenditures for continuing research programs should be disclosed separately in the income statement as a deduction from gross profit if the amounts are material. The information may sometimes be disclosed parenthetically in the income statement or in a note to the financial statements. A company should describe elsewhere in the annual report accounting policies for its continuing research program and evaluate the effectiveness of the program.

Substantial Development Projects. Projects that meet the criteria for deferral could be critical to the future profitability of a company. Since a substantial project involves a significant commitment of company funds, stockholders are entitled to an explanation of expected benefits as well as a periodic evaluation of risks. Financial analysts generally believe that "deferment should be accompanied by full disclosure of the pertinent details" to enable them to make appropriate analyses.[4]

Full disclosure would require that material amounts of deferred development costs be shown separately in the balance sheet as a noncurrent asset or disclosed in a note to the financial statements. Amortizations during the period or amounts written off as excess costs should be disclosed separately in the income statement, if material, as a deduction from gross profit.

---

[4] Morton Backer, "Financial Reporting and Security Investment Decisions," *Financial Executive*, December 1966, p. 54.

APPENDIX

**Description and Tabulated Results of
a Survey of
Accounting Practices for
Research and Development Costs**

Conducted for
the Accounting Research Division of
the American Institute of
Certified Public Accountants
September 1965

Elmo Roper and Associates

Foreword

The Accounting Research Division of the American Institute of Certified Public Accountants enlisted the aid of Elmo Roper and Associates in conducting a study of current accounting practices for research and development expenditures. Decisions concerning the basic content of the questionnaire and the companies to be included in the sample were made by the Institute. The Roper organization's function was to advise the Institute on how to pose their questions most objectively and on ways to insure a higher return rate on a mail questionnaire. In addition, the Roper organization was responsible for the coding and tabulation of the results.

The study was conducted in two waves among manufacturers that engage in substantial research or development for their own account. The first group to receive the questionnaire was "mature" companies—long standing companies which perform the bulk of company-financed industrial research and development. A mailing was made on March 15, 1965, to the top 300 "mature" companies of a list compiled by estimated size of research and development expenditures. A covering letter from the Institute explaining the purpose of the survey, and soliciting respondent cooperation, accompanied the questionnaire. Because it was felt that some companies might consider the information confidential, the questionnaire invited anonymous replies. Three weeks after the questionnaires were mailed a follow-up letter was sent to all 300 companies asking them to return the questionnaire if they had not already done so.

In the second mailing on July 6, 1965, letters and questionnaires were sent to 100 "more recently developed" companies—i.e., primarily research-oriented companies organized within the past 25 years to whom research and development may be more significant as a means of long range development. The purpose of mailing to these latter companies was to determine whether any difference of opinion might exist between this group and the long-established companies. All tabulations show separate results for companies in the first and second groups.

Two hundred and forty-five completed questionnaires were received by the Institute. (It should be noted in passing that this 61% rate of return is extremely high for a mail survey involving a questionnaire as complex and as long as the one employed in this study.) Since the great majority of the respondents chose to identify themselves, the Institute was able to be assured that the companies returning the questionnaires were not atypical of the universe sampled.

APPENDIX: RESULTS OF A SURVEY OF ACCOUNTING PRACTICES

The "free answer" questions—those requiring written answers by respondents—were reviewed by the Institute and tabulated only where the replies seemed significant (Question 25) to the purpose of the study.

In the tabulations (beginning on the next page), the "mature" companies were further subdivided for analytic purposes. The column labeled "Total" is the total of the three types of "mature companies," and does not include the "more recently developed companies." It should be noted that percentages based on small numbers of cases should be interpreted with caution since they may or may not be truly representative of the larger group from which they were drawn.

Questions 1, 2, 3

		Analyzed by respondents who are in the:			
		Mature companies			More recently developed companies
	Total	Durable goods industries	Non-durable goods industries	Diversified	

Q. 1. *Laboratory work which results in a new compound with unique and unusual properties would be initially accounted for as a cost of:*

	%	%	%	%	%
Research	86	86	87	82	72
Development	3	6	1	3	20
Both research and development	11	8	12	15	—
Manufacturing	—	—	—	—	5
Selling	—	—	—	—	—
No answer	—	—	—	—	3
	(100%)	(100%)	(100%)	(100%)	(100%)
No. of respondents	209	99	77	33	36

Q. 2. *Those who regard this function as being research or development, or both research and development, would be more likely to have such costs:*

	%	%	%	%	%
Written off	99	99	99	100	91
Deferred	1	1	—	—	9
No answer	*	—	1	—	—
	(100%)	(100%)	(100%)	(100%)	(100%)
No. of respondents	209	99	77	33	33

Q. 3. *... and would be more likely to treat such costs as:*

	%	%	%	%	%
Product costs	10	9	8	15	24
Period costs	89	91	90	85	76
Both	—	—	—	—	—
No answer	1	—	2	—	—
	(100%)	(100%)	(100%)	(100%)	(100%)
No. of respondents	209	99	77	33	33

* Less than .5 per cent

APPENDIX: RESULTS OF A SURVEY OF ACCOUNTING PRACTICES

Questions 1, 2, 3	\multicolumn{5}{c}{Analyzed by respondents who are in the:}
		Mature companies			More recently developed companies
	Total	Durable goods industries	Non-durable goods industries	Diversified	

Q. 1. *Testing all areas of uncertainty to determine whether a potential product exists would be initially accounted for as a cost of:*

	%	%	%	%	%
Research	78	82	79	61	53
Development	10	9	5	21	27
Both research and development	10	6	15	15	—
Manufacturing	—	—	—	—	3
Selling	2	3	1	—	11
No answer	*	—	—	3	6
	(100%)	(100%)	(100%)	(100%)	(100%)
No. of respondents	209	99	77	33	36

Q. 2. *Those who regard this function as being research or development, or both research and development, would be more likely to have such costs:*

	%	%	%	%	%
Written off	99	99	99	100	97
Deferred	—	—	—	—	3
No answer	1	1	1	—	—
	(100%)	(100%)	(100%)	(100%)	(100%)
No. of respondents	204	96	76	32	29

Q. 3. *... and would be more likely to treat such costs as:*

	%	%	%	%	%
Product costs	9	8	11	16	24
Period costs	90	92	89	84	76
Both	—	—	—	—	—
No answer	1	—	—	—	—
	(100%)	(100%)	(100%)	(100%)	(100%)
No. of respondents	204	96	76	32	29

* Less than .5 per cent

Questions 1, 2, 3

Analyzed by respondents who are in the:

	Total	Mature companies — Durable goods industries	Mature companies — Non-durable goods industries	Diversi- fied	More recently developed companies
Q. 1. Searching for product applications for which the new compound is suitable would be initially accounted for as a cost of:	%	%	%	%	%
Research	49	53	53	30	33
Development	33	35	27	40	33
Both research and development	10	7	13	12	—
Manufacturing	°	—	1	—	—
Selling	8	5	6	18	28
No answer	—	—	—	—	6
	(100%)	(100%)	(100%)	(100%)	(100%)
No. of respondents	209	99	77	33	36
Q. 2. Those who regard this function as being research or development, or both research and development, would be more likely to have such costs:	%	%	%	%	%
Written off	99	100	99	100	96
Deferred	—	—	—	—	4
No answer	1	—	1	—	—
	(100%)	(100%)	(100%)	(100%)	(100%)
No. of respondents	192	94	71	27	24
Q. 3. . . . and would be more likely to treat such costs as:	%	%	%	%	%
Product costs	10	9	7	19	25
Period costs	89	91	90	81	75
Both	—	—	—	—	—
No answer	1	—	3	—	—
	(100%)	(100%)	(100%)	(100%)	(100%)
No. of respondents	192	94	71	27	24

° Less than .5 per cent

APPENDIX: RESULTS OF A SURVEY OF ACCOUNTING PRACTICES

Questions 1, 2, 3	\multicolumn{5}{c}{Analyzed by respondents who are in the:}
		Mature companies			More recently developed companies
	Total	Durable goods industries	Non-durable goods industries	Diversified	

Q. 1. *Trying to modify the compound's properties to better fit a specific product application would be initially accounted for as a cost of:*

	%	%	%	%	%
Research	40	38	46	33	27
Development	46	53	36	52	61
Both research and development	11	8	12	15	—
Manufacturing	1	1	1	—	6
Selling	2	—	5	—	—
No answer	—	—	—	—	6
	(100%)	(100%)	(100%)	(100%)	(100%)
No. of respondents	209	99	77	33	36

Q. 2. *Those who regard this function as being research or development, or both research and development, would be more likely to have such costs:*

	%	%	%	%	%
Written off	100	100	99	100	97
Deferred	—	—	—	—	3
No answer	*	—	1	—	—
	(100%)	(100%)	(100%)	(100%)	(100%)
No. of respondents	203	98	72	33	32

Q. 3. *... and would be more likely to treat such costs as:*

	%	%	%	%	%
Product costs	11	8	10	21	25
Period costs	88	92	87	79	75
Both	—	—	—	—	—
No answer	1	—	3	—	—
	(100%)	(100%)	(100%)	(100%)	(100%)
No. of respondents	203	98	72	33	32

* Less than .5 per cent

Questions 1, 2, 3 — *Analyzed by respondents who are in the:*

	Total	Mature companies — Durable goods industries	Mature companies — Non-durable goods industries	Diversi-fied	More recently developed companies

Q. 1. *Development of prototypes of the product would be initially accounted for as a cost of:*

	%	%	%	%	%
Research	24	17	37	12	22
Development	62	73	43	70	67
Both research and development	11	8	13	15	—
Manufacturing	2	2	3	3	11
Selling	1	—	3	—	—
No answer	*	—	1	—	—
	(100%)	(100%)	(100%)	(100%)	(100%)
No. of respondents	209	99	77	33	36

Q. 2. *Those who regard this function as being research or development, or both research and development, would be more likely to have such costs:*

	%	%	%	%	%
Written off	97	96	99	97	81
Deferred	3	4	—	3	19
No answer	—	—	1	—	—
	(100%)	(100%)	(100%)	(100%)	(100%)
No. of respondents	201	97	72	32	32

Q. 3. *... and would be more likely to treat such costs as:*

	%	%	%	%	%
Product costs	13	12	11	19	31
Period costs	86	88	86	78	69
Both	—	—	—	—	—
No answer	1	—	3	3	—
	(100%)	(100%)	(100%)	(100%)	(100%)
No. of respondents	201	97	72	32	32

* Less than .5 per cent

APPENDIX: RESULTS OF A SURVEY OF ACCOUNTING PRACTICES

Questions 1, 2, 3 — *Analyzed by respondents who are in the:*

	Total	Mature companies — Durable goods industries	Mature companies — Non-durable goods industries	Diversified	More recently developed companies

Q. 1. *Measuring potential reactions to the product through consumer market research would be initially accounted for as a cost of:*

	%	%	%	%	%
Research	7	8	8	3	3
Development	18	15	23	9	11
Both research and development	4	3	7	—	—
Manufacturing	*	1	—	—	—
Selling	71	73	62	88	78
No answer	—	—	—	—	8
	(100%)	(100%)	(100%)	(100%)	(100%)
No. of respondents	209	99	77	33	36

Q. 2. *Those who regard this function as being research or development, or both research and development, would be more likely to have such costs:*

	%	%	%	%	%
Written off	98	100	97	100	100
Deferred	—	—	—	—	—
No answer	2	—	3	—	—
	(100%)	(100%)	(100%)	(100%)	(100%)
No. of respondents	59	26	29	4	5

Q. 3. *...and would be more likely to treat such costs as:*

	%	%	%	%	%
Product costs	7	4	7	25	20
Period costs	86	92	83	75	80
Both	2	4	—	—	—
No answer	5	—	10	—	—
	(100%)	(100%)	(100%)	(100%)	(100%)
No. of respondents	59	26	29	4	5

* Less than .5 per cent

Questions 1, 2, 3	\multicolumn{5}{c}{Analyzed by respondents who are in the:}
	\multicolumn{3}{c}{Mature companies}		More recently developed companies
	Total	Durable goods industries	Non-durable goods industries	Diversified	

Q. 1. *Design and construction of pilot plant would be initially accounted for as a cost of:*

	%	%	%	%	%
Research	15	10	20	15	11
Development	46	50	47	37	28
Both research and development	8	5	12	6	—
Manufacturing	24	29	12	36	47
Selling	*	1	—	—	—
No answer	7	5	9	6	14
	(100%)	(100%)	(100%)	(100%)	(100%)
No. of respondents	209	99	77	33	36

Q. 2. *Those who regard this function as being research or development, or both research and development, would be more likely to have such costs:*

	%	%	%	%	%
Written off	66	66	59	89	21
Deferred	30	30	38	11	79
No answer	4	4	3	—	—
	(100%)	(100%)	(100%)	(100%)	(100%)
No. of respondents	144	64	61	19	14

Q. 3. *... and would be more likely to treat such costs as:*

	%	%	%	%	%
Product costs	17	14	18	26	50
Period costs	78	82	76	74	42
Both	2	1	3	—	—
No answer	3	3	3	—	8
	(100%)	(100%)	(100%)	(100%)	(100%)
No. of respondents	144	64	61	19	14

* Less than .5 per cent

APPENDIX: RESULTS OF A SURVEY OF ACCOUNTING PRACTICES

Questions 1, 2, 3 — *Analyzed by respondents who are in the:*

	Total	Mature companies Durable goods industries	Mature companies Non-durable goods industries	Diversified	More recently developed companies

Q. 1. Pilot production would be initially accounted for as a cost of:

	%	%	%	%	%
Research	15	10	22	9	5
Development	40	39	47	30	17
Both research and development	7	5	11	—	—
Manufacturing	37	45	17	61	75
Selling	1	—	3	—	—
No answer	*	1	—	—	3
	(100%)	(100%)	(100%)	(100%)	(100%)
No. of respondents	209	99	77	33	36

Q. 2. Those who regard this function as being research or development, or both research and development, would be more likely to have such costs:

	%	%	%	%	%
Written off	94	92	95	100	75
Deferred	5	8	3	—	25
No answer	1	—	2	—	—
	(100%)	(100%)	(100%)	(100%)	(100%)
No. of respondents	128	53	62	13	8

Q. 3. ... and would be more likely to treat such costs as:

	%	%	%	%	%
Product costs	16	11	18	23	50
Period costs	78	83	76	69	50
Both	3	6	2	—	—
No answer	3	—	4	8	—
	(100%)	(100%)	(100%)	(100%)	(100%)
No. of respondents	128	53	62	13	8

* Less than .5 per cent

Questions 1, 2, 3	Analyzed by respondents who are in the:				
		Mature companies			More recently developed companies
	Total	Durable goods industries	Non-durable goods industries	Diversified	

Q. 1. *Test marketing would be initially accounted for as a cost of:*

	%	%	%	%	%
Research	2	1	2	3	3
Development	11	12	13	3	3
Both research and development	2	1	4	—	—
Manufacturing	1	1	3	—	—
Selling	83	84	78	91	86
No answer	1	1	—	3	8
	(100%)	(100%)	(100%)	(100%)	(100%)
No. of respondents	209	99	77	33	36

Q. 2. *Those who regard this function as being research or development, or both research and development, would be more likely to have such costs:*

	%	%	%	%	%
Written off	100	100	100	100	50
Deferred	—	—	—	—	50
No answer	—	—	—	—	—
	(100%)	(100%)	(100%)	(100%)	(100%)
No. of respondents	31	14	15	2	2

Q. 3. *... and would be more likely to treat such costs as:*

	%	%	%	%	%
Product costs	6	—	13	—	—
Period costs	88	100	74	100	100
Both	—	—	—	—	—
No answer	6	—	13	—	—
	(100%)	(100%)	(100%)	(100%)	(100%)
No. of respondents	31	14	15	2	2

APPENDIX: RESULTS OF A SURVEY OF ACCOUNTING PRACTICES

Questions 1, 2, 3

Analyzed by respondents who are in the:

	Total	Mature companies — Durable goods industries	Mature companies — Non-durable goods industries	Diversified	More recently developed companies

Q. 1. *Using research personnel to help set up initial production runs would be initially accounted for as a cost of:*

	%	%	%	%	%
Research	18	16	22	15	8
Development	34	34	31	37	36
Both research and development	7	6	8	9	—
Manufacturing	41	44	38	39	53
Selling	*	—	1	—	—
No answer	—	—	—	—	3
	(100%)	(100%)	(100%)	(100%)	(100%)
No. of respondents	209	99	77	33	36

Q. 2. *Those who regard this function as being research or development, or both research and development, would be more likely to have such costs:*

	%	%	%	%	%
Written off	97	96	100	95	75
Deferred	1	2	—	—	19
No answer	2	2	—	5	6
	(100%)	(100%)	(100%)	(100%)	(100%)
No. of respondents	123	56	47	20	16

Q. 3. *... and would be more likely to treat such costs as:*

	%	%	%	%	%
Product costs	15	11	15	30	38
Period costs	81	84	83	65	56
Both	1	2	—	—	—
No answer	3	3	2	5	6
	(100%)	(100%)	(100%)	(100%)	(100%)
No. of respondents	123	56	47	20	16

* Less than .5 per cent

Question 1

	Analyzed by respondents who are in the:				
		Mature companies			More
		Durable	Non-durable		recently
		goods	goods	Diversi-	developed
	Total	industries	industries	fied	companies

Q. 1. *Operating production line quality controls when product is in full-scale production would be initially accounted for as a cost of:*

	%	%	%	%	%
Research	—	—	—	—	—
Development	—	—	—	—	—
Both research and development	—	—	—	—	—
Manufacturing	99	100	97	100	97
Selling	1	—	3	—	—
No answer	—	—	—	—	3
	(100%)	(100%)	(100%)	(100%)	(100%)
No. of respondents	209	99	77	33	36

NOTE: Questions 2 and 3 not shown because no respondent considered this function to be research and/or development.

APPENDIX: RESULTS OF A SURVEY OF ACCOUNTING PRACTICES

Q. 4. Example A

The project will take *4-6 years* from the inception of the research to full-scale production.

The project's research and development expenditures will absorb *20%* of the company's annual research and development budget for each of the 4-6 years. The annual research and development budget is equal to *50%* of the company's annual income before taxes.

The product has *one chance in ten* of being a commercial success (although with high profitability if it succeeds).

	Analyzed by respondents who are in the:				
		Mature companies			*More*
		Durable	*Non-durable*		*recently*
		goods	*goods*	*Diversi-*	*developed*
	Total	*industries*	*industries*	*fied*	*companies*

a. *According to accounting theory the research and development costs of this project should be:*

	%	%	%	%	%
Written off	93	96	92	88	92
Deferred	4	3	3	6	8
No answer	3	1	5	6	—

b. *Recognizing the practical problems involved, the research and development costs probably would be:*

	%	%	%	%	%
Written off	97	99	94	97	97
Deferred	*	—	—	3	3
No answer	3	1	6	—	—
	(100%)	(100%)	(100%)	(100%)	(100%)
No. of respondents	209	99	77	33	36

* Less than .5 per cent

Q. 4. Example B

The project will take *4-6 years* from the inception of the research to full-scale production.

The project's research and development expenditures will absorb *20%* of the company's annual research and development budget for each of the 4-6 years. The annual research and development budget is equal to *50%* of the company's annual income before taxes.

The product has *nine chances in ten* of being a commercial success.

	\multicolumn{4}{c}{Analyzed by respondents who are in the:}	
		Mature companies			More recently developed companies
	Total	Durable goods industries	Non-durable goods industries	Diversified	

a. According to accounting theory the research and development costs of this project should be:

	%	%	%	%	%
Written off	67	69	70	55	61
Deferred	29	29	25	39	39
No answer	4	2	5	6	—

b. Recognizing the practical problems involved, the research and development costs probably would be:

	%	%	%	%	%
Written off	87	89	87	79	86
Deferred	11	11	8	21	14
No answer	2	—	5	—	—
	(100%)	(100%)	(100%)	(100%)	(100%)
No. of respondents	209	99	77	33	36

APPENDIX: RESULTS OF A SURVEY OF ACCOUNTING PRACTICES

Q. 4. Example C

The project will take *2 years* from the inception of the research to full-scale production.

The project's research and development expenditures will absorb *20%* of the company's annual research and development budget for each of the 2 years. The annual research and development budget is equal to *50%* of the company's annual income before taxes.

The product has *nine chances in ten* of being a commercial success.

	\multicolumn{5}{c}{Analyzed by respondents who are in the:}
		\multicolumn{3}{c}{Mature companies}	More recently developed companies
	Total	Durable goods industries	Non-durable goods industries	Diversified	

a. *According to accounting theory the research and development costs of this project should be:*

	%	%	%	%	%
Written off	69	71	70	61	58
Deferred	27	27	23	33	42
No answer	4	2	7	6	—

b. *Recognizing the practical problems involved, the research and development costs probably would be:*

	%	%	%	%	%
Written off	86	89	83	82	81
Deferred	12	11	12	18	19
No answer	2	—	5	—	—
	(100%)	(100%)	(100%)	(100%)	(100%)
No. of respondents	209	99	77	33	36

Q. 4. Example D

The project will take *10 years* from the inception of the research to full-scale production.

The project's research and development expenditures will absorb *20%* of the company's annual research and development budget for each of the 10 years. The annual research and development budget is equal to *50%* of the company's annual income before taxes.

The product has *nine chances in ten* of being a commercial success.

		Analyzed by respondents who are in the:			
		Mature companies			More recently developed companies
	Total	Durable goods industries	Non-durable goods industries	Diversified	

a. *According to accounting theory the research and development costs of this project should be:*

	%	%	%	%	%
Written off	70	70	74	61	69
Deferred	25	27	20	33	31
No answer	5	3	6	6	—

b. *Recognizing the practical problems involved, the research and development costs probably would be:*

	%	%	%	%	%
Written off	87	90	86	82	92
Deferred	11	9	9	18	8
No answer	2	1	5	—	—
	(100%)	(100%)	(100%)	(100%)	(100%)
No. of respondents	209	99	77	33	36

APPENDIX: RESULTS OF A SURVEY OF ACCOUNTING PRACTICES

Q. 4. Example E

The project will take *4-6 years* from the inception of the research to full-scale production.

The project's research and development expenditures will absorb 5% of the company's annual research and development budget for each of the 4-6 years. The annual research and development budget is equal to 20% of the company's annual income before taxes.

The product has *nine chances in ten* of being a commercial success.

	Analyzed by respondents who are in the:				
		Mature companies			*More recently developed companies*
	Total	*Durable goods industries*	*Non-durable goods industries*	*Diversified*	

a. *According to accounting theory the research and development costs of this project should be:*

	%	%	%	%	%
Written off	78	77	82	76	81
Deferred	17	21	12	15	19
No answer	5	2	6	9	—

b. *Recognizing the practical problems involved, the research and development costs probably would be:*

	%	%	%	%	%
Written off	94	95	94	91	94
Deferred	5	5	2	9	6
No answer	1	—	4	—	—
	(100%)	(100%)	(100%)	(100%)	(100%)
No. of respondents	209	99	77	33	36

Q. 4. Example F

The project will take *4-6 years* from the inception of the research to full-scale production.

The project's research and development expenditures will absorb *40%* of the company's annual research and development budget for each of the 4-6 years. The annual research and development budget is equal to *50%* of the company's annual income before taxes.

The product has *nine chances in ten* of being a commercial success.

	Total	Analyzed by respondents who are in the:			More recently developed companies
		Mature companies			
		Durable goods industries	Non-durable goods industries	Diversi- fied	

a. *According to accounting theory the research and development costs of this project should be:*

	%	%	%	%	%
Written off	66	67	69	55	61
Deferred	29	30	25	36	39
No answer	5	3	6	9	—

b. *Recognizing the practical problems involved, the research and development costs probably would be:*

	%	%	%	%	%
Written off	83	87	83	73	86
Deferred	15	12	12	27	14
No answer	2	1	5	—	—
	(100%)	(100%)	(100%)	(100%)	(100%)
No. of respondents	209	99	77	33	36

APPENDIX: RESULTS OF A SURVEY OF ACCOUNTING PRACTICES

Q. 4. Example G

The project will take *4-6 years* from the inception of the research to full-scale production.

The project's research and development expenditures will absorb 20% of the company's annual research and development budget for each of the 4-6 years. The annual research and development budget is equal to 50% of the company's annual income before taxes.

The product has *five chances in ten* of being a commercial success.

	Analyzed by respondents who are in the:				
		Mature companies			*More recently developed companies*
	Total	*Durable goods industries*	*Non-durable goods industries*	*Diversified*	
a. *According to accounting theory the research and development costs of this project should be:*					
	%	%	%	%	%
Written off	88	90	85	88	83
Deferred	8	8	9	3	17
No answer	4	2	6	9	—
b. *Recognizing the practical problems involved, the research and development costs probably would be:*					
	%	%	%	%	%
Written off	96	98	92	97	94
Deferred	2	2	3	3	6
No answer	2	—	5	—	—
	(100%)	(100%)	(100%)	(100%)	(100%)
No. of respondents	209	99	77	33	36

Q. 6. Budgeted research and development expenditures have been viewed as being needed for future expansion and growth as well as for maintenance of a competitive position in the industry. Which of the following comes closest to the way it is viewed by your company?

	Analyzed by respondents who are in the:				
		Mature companies			*More recently developed companies*
	Total	*Durable goods industries*	*Non-durable goods industries*	*Diversified*	
	%	%	%	%	%
Almost wholly as necessary for expansion and growth	4	6	3	3	17
More for expansion and growth than for maintenance of a competitive position	18	11	27	15	25
About equally for growth and to maintain competitive position	63	64	58	70	53
More for maintenance of competitive position than for growth	13	16	12	9	5
Almost wholly to maintain a competitive position	2	3	—	3	—
	(100%)	(100%)	(100%)	(100%)	(100%)
No. of respondents	209	99	77	33	36

Q. 7. Would you say, based on your experience, that research that is not successful in achieving its intended objectives leads to unexpected benefits very often, occasionally, rarely, or never?

	Analyzed by respondents who are in the:				
		Mature companies			*More recently developed companies*
	Total	*Durable goods industries*	*Non-durable goods industries*	*Diversified*	
	%	%	%	%	%
Very often	9	10	3	18	8
Occasionally	56	54	71	27	64
Rarely	32	34	23	46	28
Never	—	—	—	—	—
No answer	3	2	3	9	—
	(100%)	(100%)	(100%)	(100%)	(100%)
No. of respondents	209	99	77	33	36

APPENDIX: RESULTS OF A SURVEY OF ACCOUNTING PRACTICES

Q. 8. From a long-range planning point of view, at the time a research project begins, do you always, occasionally, rarely, or never attempt to predict the future years of time periods during which benefits of the project will be realized?

	Analyzed by respondents who are in the:				
		Mature companies			*More recently developed companies*
	Total	Durable goods industries	Non-durable goods industries	Diversified	
	%	%	%	%	%
Always	47	51	43	49	58
Occasionally	34	34	35	30	19
Rarely	13	10	17	12	17
Never	3	3	4	3	6
No answer	3	2	1	6	—
	(100%)	(100%)	(100%)	(100%)	(100%)
No. of respondents	209	99	77	33	36

Q. 9. Based on past experience, about what percentage of your *research* expenditures would you say are identifiable with projects which result in commercially successful products?

Per cent	*Analyzed by respondents who are in the:*				
		Mature companies			*More recently developed companies*
	Total	Durable goods industries	Non-durable goods industries	Diversified	
	%	%	%	%	%
1 to 10	21	18	27	15	25
11 to 20	13	12	14	15	8
21 to 30	15	23	8	9	14
31 to 40	4	6	3	—	3
41 to 50	8	11	4	6	16
51 to 60	3	5	1	—	—
61 to 70	1	1	1	3	—
71 to 80	3	3	3	6	3
81 to 90	2	4	—	3	—
91 to 100	1	1	—	—	3
Don't know	9	5	10	15	—
No answer	20	11	29	28	28
	(100%)	(100%)	(100%)	(100%)	(100%)
No. of respondents	209	99	77	33	36

Q. 10. Based on past experience, about what percentage of your *development* expenditures would you say are identifiable with projects which result in commercially successful products?

	Analyzed by respondents who are in the:				
		Mature companies			More recently developed companies
		Durable goods industries	Non-durable goods industries	Diversified	
Per cent	Total				
	%	%	%	%	%
1 to 10	5	3	9	3	3
11 to 20	3	4	4	—	5
21 to 30	8	6	8	12	17
31 to 40	5	7	4	—	8
41 to 50	12	15	9	9	14
51 to 60	9	11	8	6	—
61 to 70	4	3	4	6	11
71 to 80	15	20	6	18	19
81 to 90	9	11	9	3	3
91 to 100	3	5	—	6	6
Don't know	7	4	9	12	—
No answer	20	11	30	25	14
	(100%)	(100%)	(100%)	(100%)	(100%)
No. of respondents	209	99	77	33	36

Q. 11. From the standpoint of your company philosophy, are current revenues intended to cover the cost of research and development on new products, or is the revenue from the new products intended to absorb the related research and development costs?

	Analyzed by respondents who are in the:				
		Mature companies			More recently developed companies
		Durable goods industries	Non-durable goods industries	Diversified	
	Total				
	%	%	%	%	%
Current product revenues cover costs	93	96	88	94	89
New product revenues cover costs	6	4	9	6	11
No answer	1	—	3	—	—
	(100%)	(100%)	(100%)	(100%)	(100%)
No. of respondents	209	99	77	33	36

APPENDIX: RESULTS OF A SURVEY OF ACCOUNTING PRACTICES

Q. 12. For internal reporting purposes, do you always, sometimes, or never allocate indirect research and development costs as overhead to specific projects?

	Analyzed by respondents who are in the:				
		Mature companies			More recently developed companies
		Durable goods industries	Non-durable goods industries	Diversi- fied	
	Total				
	%	%	%	%	%
Always	51	48	60	40	25
Sometimes	15	15	12	21	19
Never	33	36	26	39	56
No answer	1	1	2	—	—
	(100%)	(100%)	(100%)	(100%)	(100%)
No. of respondents	209	99	77	33	36

Q. 13. Do you always, sometimes, or never include some general or administrative overhead in research and development costs?

	Analyzed by respondents who are in the:				
		Mature companies			More recently developed companies
		Durable goods industries	Non-durable goods industries	Diversi- fied	
	Total				
	%	%	%	%	%
Always	18	14	25	12	19
Sometimes	13	16	10	9	11
Never	69	70	65	79	70
	(100%)	(100%)	(100%)	(100%)	(100%)
No. of respondents	209	99	77	33	36

Q. 14a. It has been said that "the immediate write-off of research and development expenditures is far from economic reality." Do you generally agree or disagree with this statement?

	Total	Analyzed by respondents who are in the:			More recently developed companies
		Mature companies			
		Durable goods industries	Non-durable goods industries	Diversified	
	%	%	%	%	%
Agree	25	22	25	36	33
Disagree	73	75	74	64	67
No answer	2	3	1	—	—
	(100%)	(100%)	(100%)	(100%)	(100%)
No. of respondents	209	99	77	33	36

Q. 14b. It has also been said that "as a matter of conservatism, however, such expenditures should be written off as incurred." Do you generally agree or disagree with this position?

	Total	Analyzed by respondents who are in the:			More recently developed companies
		Mature companies			
		Durable goods industries	Non-durable goods industries	Diversified	
	%	%	%	%	%
Agree	91	94	88	91	92
Disagree	7	5	8	9	8
No answer	2	1	4	—	—
	(100%)	(100%)	(100%)	(100%)	(100%)
No. of respondents	209	99	77	33	36

APPENDIX: RESULTS OF A SURVEY OF ACCOUNTING PRACTICES

Q. 15. Does the expensing of research and development expenditures as incurred create considerable, little, or no difficulty in evaluating the profit performance of a company?

	Analyzed by respondents who are in the:				
		Mature companies			*More*
		Durable	*Non-durable*		*recently*
		goods	*goods*	*Diversi-*	*developed*
	Total	*industries*	*industries*	*fied*	*companies*
	%	%	%	%	%
Considerable effect	10	10	9	9	28
Little effect	62	63	60	64	44
No effect	25	24	27	24	25
No answer	3	3	4	3	3
	(100%)	(100%)	(100%)	(100%)	(100%)
No. of respondents	209	99	77	33	36

Q. 16. If research and development expenditures are deferred to future years, how should unsuccessful research be handled: should it be written off just as soon as the failure becomes evident, or should it be continued as a deferral allocable to successful research?

	Analyzed by respondents who are in the:				
		Mature companies			*More*
		Durable	*Non-durable*		*recently*
		goods	*goods*	*Diversi-*	*developed*
	Total	*industries*	*industries*	*fied*	*companies*
	%	%	%	%	%
Written off	92	88	96	97	92
Continued as deferral	3	5	1	—	5
No answer	5	7	3	3	3
	(100%)	(100%)	(100%)	(100%)	(100%)
No. of respondents	209	99	77	33	36

Q. 17. Do you think it is always appropriate, sometimes appropriate, or never appropriate to defer research and development expenditures connected with: a new company; a new product division; expanding the uses of an existing product?

		Analyzed by respondents who are in the:			
		Mature companies			More recently developed companies
	Total	Durable goods industries	Non-durable goods industries	Diversi- fied	
a. A new company	%	%	%	%	%
Always	7	7	5	12	14
Sometimes	65	67	66	61	47
Never	26	26	26	24	36
No answer	2	—	3	3	3
b. A new product division of an existing company	%	%	%	%	%
Always	3	2	1	9	8
Sometimes	49	51	49	42	45
Never	47	47	47	49	44
No answer	1	—	3	—	3
c. Expanding uses of an existing product	%	%	%	%	%
Always	2	1	—	6	—
Sometimes	19	16	25	15	14
Never	78	83	73	79	83
No answer	1	—	2	—	3
	(100%)	(100%)	(100%)	(100%)	(100%)
No. of respondents	209	99	77	33	36

APPENDIX: RESULTS OF A SURVEY OF ACCOUNTING PRACTICES

Q. 18a. Would you consider it appropriate to charge off currently the research and development expenditures required to maintain a business in a competitive position while at the same time deferring such expenditures connected with expanding a business?

		Analyzed by respondents who are in the:			
		Mature companies			More
		Durable	Non-durable		recently
		goods	goods	Diversi-	developed
	Total	industries	industries	fied	companies
	%	%	%	%	%
Yes	25	25	26	21	39
No	74	74	72	79	56
No answer	1	1	2	—	5
	(100%)	(100%)	(100%)	(100%)	(100%)
No. of respondents	209	99	77	33	36

Q. 18b. Would you consider it appropriate to charge off currently recurring research and development expenditures while at the same time deferring extraordinary expenditures on special projects?

		Analyzed by respondents who are in the:			
		Mature companies			More
		Durable	Non-durable		recently
		goods	goods	Diversi-	developed
	Total	industries	industries	fied	companies
	%	%	%	%	%
Yes	44	40	46	52	42
No	54	58	52	48	58
No answer	2	2	2	—	—
	(100%)	(100%)	(100%)	(100%)	(100%)
No. of respondents	209	99	77	33	36

Q. 19. Do you think there is any less reason to capitalize the cost of a company's own research than the cost of purchased research?

		Analyzed by respondents who are in the:			
		Mature companies			More
		Durable	Non-durable		recently
		goods	goods	Diversi-	developed
	Total	industries	industries	fied	companies
	%	%	%	%	%
Yes	11	9	13	15	6
No	86	88	85	82	89
No answer	3	3	2	3	5
	(100%)	(100%)	(100%)	(100%)	(100%)
No. of respondents	209	99	77	33	36

Q. 20. In acquiring another company, where research is part of the consideration for purchase, would there be good reason to capitalize the portion of the excess cost attributable to research and development even though the acquired company may have previously written off research and development expenditures?

		Analyzed by respondents who are in the:			
		Mature companies			More
		Durable	Non-durable		recently
		goods	goods	Diversi-	developed
	Total	industries	industries	fied	companies
	%	%	%	%	%
Yes	54	53	60	43	47
No	42	45	39	42	47
No answer	4	2	1	15	6
	(100%)	(100%)	(100%)	(100%)	(100%)
No. of respondents	209	99	77	33	36

APPENDIX: RESULTS OF A SURVEY OF ACCOUNTING PRACTICES

Q. 21. Do you think it would be appropriate to provide annually for research and development expenditures by establishing a reserve (based, say, on some percentage of sales) against which actual expenditures would be charged?

		Analyzed by respondents who are in the:			
		Mature companies			*More*
		Durable	*Non-durable*		*recently*
		goods	*goods*	*Diversi-*	*developed*
	Total	*industries*	*industries*	*fied*	*companies*
	%	%	%	%	%
Yes	24	25	24	21	31
No	76	75	75	79	69
No answer	*	—	1	—	—
	(100%)	(100%)	(100%)	(100%)	(100%)
No. of respondents	209	99	77	33	36

* Less than .5 per cent

Q. 22. Which of the following does your company do with respect to disclosing its annual research and development expenditures?

		Analyzed by respondents who are in the:			
		Mature companies			More recently developed companies
	Total	Durable goods industries	Non-durable goods industries	Diversified	
	%	%	%	%	%
a. They are presented in the income statement as a functional classification	18	13	23	18	28
b. They are presented in a footnote to the financial statement	*	—	1	—	6
c. They are presented elsewhere in the annual report	31	31	31	30	14
d. They are presented in speeches or press releases	33	17	22	12	—
e. Company does not now disclose R&D expenditures	40	44	32	42	53
	(100%)	(100%)	(100%)	(100%)	(100%)
No. of respondents	209	99	77	33	36

* Less than .5 per cent

NOTE: Percentages add to more than 100% because some respondents gave more than one answer.

APPENDIX: RESULTS OF A SURVEY OF ACCOUNTING PRACTICES

Q. 23. Although you do not *now* disclose research and development expenditures, would you favor the general practice of disclosing such expenditures in some manner?

		Analyzed by respondents who are in the:			
		Mature companies			More recently developed companies
	Total	Durable goods industries	Non-durable goods industries	Diversified	
	%	%	%	%	%
Yes, would favor	30	32	28	29	37
No, would not favor	68	66	68	71	63
No answer	2	2	4	—	—
	(100%)	(100%)	(100%)	(100%)	(100%)
No. of respondents	83	44	25	14	19

Q. 24. Although you do not *now* disclose amounts in your *income statement*, would you favor the general practice of disclosing such amounts in the income statement?

		Analyzed by respondents who are in the:			
		Mature companies			More recently developed companies
	Total	Durable goods industries	Non-durable goods industries	Diversified	
	%	%	%	%	%
Yes, would favor	40	47	32	41	64
No, would not favor	57	48	68	59	36
No answer	3	5	—	—	—
	(100%)	(100%)	(100%)	(100%)	(100%)
No. of respondents	114	56	41	17	14

Q. 25. What are your objections to disclosure of research and development expenditures in your income statement?

	Total	Mature companies Durable goods industries	Mature companies Non-durable goods industries	Diversified	More recently developed companies
	%	%	%	%	%
Definitional problem, difficult to distinguish between research and development	34	27	33	55	12
This information more helpful to competition than to stockholders; discloses private company information	33	38	22	45	35
Would be misleading; investor would not understand the figure	31	32	29	35	29
Company's business not important to investors, they're not interested	9	9	11	5	—
Figure doesn't indicate future value of the research	5	2	6	10	—
No comparability between unrelated industries	3	4	4	—	12
Other	15	11	24	5	11
No answer	5	3	6	5	5
	(100%)	(100%)	(100%)	(100%)	(100%)
No. of respondents	121	56	45	20	17

NOTE: Percentages add to more than 100% because some respondents gave more than one answer.

APPENDIX: RESULTS OF A SURVEY OF ACCOUNTING PRACTICES

Q. 26. Do your company's financial statements (or their footnotes) now indicate the *basis* of accounting for annual research and development expenditures?

and if "no,"

Q. 27. Would you favor your company indicating the basis of accounting for annual research and development expenditures in your financial statements (or their footnotes)?

		Analyzed by respondents who are in the:			
		Mature companies			More recently developed companies
	Total	Durable goods industries	Non-durable goods industries	Diversified	
	%	%	%	%	%
Yes, company's financial statements now indicate basis of accounting for annual research and development expenditures	10	12	6	9	17
No, company's financial statements do not now indicate basis of accounting for annual research and development expenditures	89	88	93	88	83
No . . . but I would favor this practice	37	36	37	39	53
No . . . and I would not favor this practice	52	52	56	49	30
No answer	1	—	1	3	—
	(100%)	(100%)	(100%)	(100%)	(100%)
No. of respondents	209	99	77	33	36

111

Q. 29a. Suppose that research is defined as the effort incurred up to the point where production proves technically feasible, and development as everything from that point up to the beginning of full production. Given that definition, one approach that has been suggested is to write off *all* of the "research" expenditures and defer *all* of the "development" expenditures. Would you generally agree or disagree with this approach?

	Total	*Analyzed by respondents who are in the:*			More recently developed companies
		Mature companies			
		Durable goods industries	Non-durable goods industries	Diversified	
	%	%	%	%	%
Agree	8	5	7	21	19
Disagree	91	95	92	79	81
No answer	1	—	1	—	—
	(100%)	(100%)	(100%)	(100%)	(100%)
No. of respondents	209	99	77	33	36

Q. 29b. Do you generally agree or not with the distinctions between research and development as stated in part "a" of this question?

	Total	*Analyzed by respondents who are in the:*			More recently developed companies
		Mature companies			
		Durable goods industries	Non-durable goods industries	Diversified	
	%	%	%	%	%
Agree with definition in part "a"	60	60	62	55	72
Disagree with definition in part "a"	39	40	35	42	25
No answer	1	—	3	3	3
	(100%)	(100%)	(100%)	(100%)	(100%)
No. of respondents	209	99	77	33	36

APPENDIX: RESULTS OF A SURVEY OF ACCOUNTING PRACTICES

Q. 30. How would you characterize your company's expenditures for research and development over the past several years? Have they been (a) relatively stable, (b) steadily increasing, (c) steadily decreasing, (d) moving up and down with sales, (e) moving up and down with net income or (f) of no discernible pattern?

		Analyzed by respondents who are in the:			
		Mature companies			More recently developed companies
	Total	Durable goods industries	Non-durable goods industries	Diversified	
	%	%	%	%	%
Stable	20	22	14	27	17
Increasing	74	72	79	70	58
Decreasing	*	1	—	—	2
Up and down with sales	1	1	1	—	3
Up and down with net income	1	2	—	—	6
No pattern	2	1	2	3	14
No answer	2	1	4	—	—
	(100%)	(100%)	(100%)	(100%)	(100%)
No. of respondents	209	99	77	33	36

* Less than .5 per cent

Q. 31. What was the approximate ratio of your company's annual expenditure on research and development in the last fiscal year to that of ten years ago?

	Total	Mature companies — Durable goods industries	Mature companies — Non-durable goods industries	Diversified	More recently developed companies
	%	%	%	%	%
1 to 1	15	16	7	27	8
2 to 1	30	20	45	27	22
3 to 1	16	20	10	16	11
4 to 1	10	10	13	3	5
5 to 1	6	8	3	9	3
6 to 1	1	1	—	6	3
7 to 1	1	1	1	—	—
8 to 1	1	2	1	—	—
10 to 1	4	6	3	—	3
Over 10 to 1	3	7	—	—	12
Don't know	4	3	4	6	—
No answer	9	6	13	6	33
	(100%)	(100%)	(100%)	(100%)	(100%)
No. of respondents	209	99	77	33	36

Selected Bibliography

AMERICAN ASSOCIATION FOR THE ADVANCEMENT OF SCIENCE. Publication No. 56, *Symposium on Basic Research.* Washington, D. C.: American Association for the Advancement of Science, 1959.

ANTHONY, ROBERT N. *Management Controls in Industrial Research Organizations.* Cambridge, Mass.: Harvard University Press, 1952.

BLAKE, MATTHEW F. "Accounting for Research and Development Costs." *New York Certified Public Accountant,* January 1959, pp. 32-46.

BRIGHT, JAMES R., Editor. *Technological Planning on the Corporate Level—Proceedings of a Conference.* Cambridge, Mass.: Harvard University Press, 1962.

BRIGHT, JAMES R. *Research, Development, and Technological Innovation.* Homewood, Ill.: Richard D. Irwin, Inc., 1964.

CONANT, JAMES B. *Science and Common Sense.* New Haven, Conn.: Yale University Press, 1951.

FURNAS, C. C. *Research in Industry.* New York: D. Van Nostrand Company, Inc., 1948.

GILFILLAN, S. C. *Invention and the Patent System.* Washington, D. C.: U. S. Government Printing Office, 1964.

HIGGINS, THOMAS G. "Deferral vs. Charge-Off of Research and Development Costs." *1954 Annual Meeting Papers.* New York: American Institute of [Certified Public] Accountants, 1954, pp. 4-17.

McGRAW-HILL PUBLICATIONS' ECONOMICS DEPARTMENT. *Business' Plans for Research and Development Expenditures 1972-1975.* New York: McGraw-Hill, May 5, 1972.

MEES, C.E.K., and LEERMAKERS, J. A. *The Organization of Industrial Scientific Research.* New York: McGraw-Hill Book Company, Inc., 1950.

NATIONAL ASSOCIATION OF ACCOUNTANTS. *Research Report No. 29, "Accounting for Research and Development Costs."* New York: NAA, 1955.

NATIONAL BUREAU OF ECONOMIC RESEARCH. *The Rate and Direction of Inventive Activity.* Princeton, N. J.: Princeton University Press, 1962.

NATIONAL INDUSTRIAL CONFERENCE BOARD. Studies in Business Economics, No. 82, *Research and Development: Its Growth and Composition.* New York: The Conference Board, Inc., 1963.

NATIONAL SCIENCE FOUNDATION. *Research and Development in Industry, 1970.* Washington, D. C.: U. S. Government Printing Office, September 1972.

NELSON, RICHARD R. "The Economics of Invention: A Survey of the Literature." *The Journal of Business,* April 1959, pp. 101-127.

NELSON, RICHARD R.; PECK, MERTON J.; and KALACHEK, EDWARD D. *Technology, Economic Growth, and Public Policy.* Washington, D. C.: The Brookings Institution, 1967.

NORTHROP, F.S.C. *The Logic of the Sciences and the Humanities.* New York: The Macmillan Company, 1947.

NORTON, L. N. "Research, Development and Other Preproduction Costs." *The Cost Accountant* (England), March 1962, pp. 72-88.

NOVICK, DAVID. "What Do We Mean By Research and Development?" *Illinois Business Review,* November 1959, pp. 6-8.

POWELL, WELDON. "New Approach to Research and Experimental Costs." *Proceedings of 13th Annual Institute on Federal Taxation.* New York: New York University Press, 1955, pp. 1015-1027.

ROSSMAN, JOSEPH. *Industrial Creativity—the psychology of the inventor.* New Hyde Park, N. Y.: University Books, Inc., 1964.

TAYLOR, CALVIN W., and BARROW F., Editors. *Scientific Creativity: Its Recognition and Development.* New York: John Wiley & Sons, Inc., 1963.

TYBOUT, RICHARD A., Editor. *Economics of Research and Development.* Columbus: Ohio State University Press, 1965.

U. S. HOUSE OF REPRESENTATIVES. *Report of the Select Committee on Government Research,* Studies 1 to 10. Washington, D. C.: U. S. Government Printing Office, 1964.

U. S. SENATE. Hearings Before the Subcommittee on Antitrust and Monopoly of the Committee on the Judiciary. *Administered Prices in the Drug Industry.* Washington, D. C.: U. S. Government Printing Office, 1960.

U. S. SENATE. Hearings Before the Subcommittee on Antitrust and Monopoly of the Committee on the Judiciary. *Part 3—Concentration, Invention, and Innovation.* Washington, D. C.: U. S. Government Printing Office, 1965.